12

* rust back root is planing sa
reach to the end of layers if surfacin
a descended flex to ...
planar spreading ties a form to ...
of flood break one front vertic

Also by Peter Larkin

Enclosures
Prose Woods
Pastoral Advert
Terrain Seed Scarcity
Slights Agreeing Trees
Sprout Near Severing Close
Rings Resting The Circuit
What the Surfaces Enclave of Wang Wei
Leaves of Field

Wordsworth and Coleridge: Promising Losses

PETER LARKIN

Lessways Least Scarce Among

Poems 2002–2009

Shearsman Books

Published in the United Kingdom in 2012 by
Shearsman Books Ltd
50 Westons Hill Drive
Emersons Green
Bristol
BS16 7DF

Shearsman Books Ltd Registered Office
30–31 St. James Place, Mangotsfield, Bristol BS16 9JB
(this address not for correspondence)

www.shearsman.com

ISBN 978-1-84861-242-6

Preface

The "scarce" word can easily seem so much small change in my writings, however equivocal it has proved or however plurivocal I might like it to be. I hope it's clear it's not a minimalist tag because to treat with what is scarce as unsubstitutable rather than just a designed infrequency requires a certain textual extravagance (which will in part be theatrical or hymnic) to winnow out what is both less than and the one thing without which. The lessened risks a failure of relation but offers its own subspecies on behalf of. The scarce is not a naturalism or elegiac realism but an incidence of damage which riskily ups the stakes on offer, that is, takes up the stakes (deliberately tree-like) to redeploy a less than holistic circuit (broken givens) in a field of more than the whole. Such givens beckon to a rarity-insight (rather than value) by not expressing gift in their own terms or as any additive form of themselves: rather, a certain subtraction (historically and ecologically real) impels the less-than to become overdetermined, so that it is no longer living within its means. A scarcity of relation doesn't effectively bask in the shuttle of detached plenitudes opaquely speculative of the world: where a meaning does occur it does so as gift and event, and so as unconditional but slighted.

This is to push naturalism to the crisis of being open to what is unaccountably less than itself (the pastoral difference), not reductively but as a charged (therefore burdened) site of the given-to (the charge not plenitudinous but wholly exceptional). If a giftless world should at last bring us the ordinary (Nancy), a gifted one plies amid the scarcity and fragility of the non-ordinary. Why should it be scarce? Because the latter can't be included among the permutations of givens (which as permutations tend to neutralise) in any other way, and this is a way to indicate receptiveness, openness to what isn't a self-similar plethora. All it can do is work at the chafed difference between givens and what gives without collapsing the necessary paucity of mediation, so as to be a work of inflection not determination, givens tapered along the tail of gift.

So, static contortions and abraded obstructions can well contribute to the grain of a singularity which at the same time summons the intimate unblendings of horizon (the desire of limit more othering than difference because on behalf of). This making scarce over a wide perspective is in ontological deference to the micro-stiffnesses of the finite, and it is these which in falling behind or below do inflect it, so that finitude on the slight side of itself (no self-sufficient diminution) mainly breaks off at its vertical taper. The prolific in ordinary might prefer to defer to the interfused commonality of the scarcely most alive. At this point traps and temptations do really diminish the scope of the scarce, which is why my language itself needs to refrain from austerity *per se.*

There can be ways in which what is scarce is not withheld at all, which is why some of the texts here show a renewed interest in the quantum verticality of trees or the willingness of horizons to stretch out surfaces just where those surfaces are not so much at risk of being intercepted as of being invited to something other than a sumptuous refolding (however formally differential): this is the poverty of not affording the relation but offering it, reaching to where there is no predetermined interruption but only singular eruption, dedication. The fraught rarities of scarcity have no way of buying off finitude but pay into it as what no longer simply elates the sum of that finitude's own differences. The world's abundant nothings are creatively slightened to "as nothing" in the face of promise, an on behalf of, or more exactly, incommensurate givens receptively less than their own (unpossessing) origin. What is scarce can be lived out as a compression of the ontological (lessways have that adverbial tinge) but is the very opposite of a contraction: no longer least where intensely among and not just sacrificial slights but more festive for tenuous.

Peter Larkin
Kenilworth
January 2010

Slights Agreeing Trees

2002

The limits have wintered me
as if white trees were there to be written on

FANNY HOWE

Distance
Dappled with diminish'd trees

GERARD MANLEY HOPKINS

A desert
walled by forest

JOHN KINSELLA

Uncertain that the world is wooded impartially

LYN HEJINIAN

1

Turf Hill

Some livery to simplify a real shank through the wards, power-lines at a slope of conduction with rapid incomplete owing of ground. To blow with spreading on the grid some green flutter of smaller rigid body.

Not covert and long not to be covered in links of shadow, a joined way lifts itself into fringe. The pylon avenue isn't corridor pulse interceding with plantation, but ventilation as if by air-arc of the horizons within clump. To displenish beside refreshed ground, what is healed and hugs shaft but never swings anew upon line-break. Grit at the big branch, anti-tentacular of hung community, but generously ferned.

How the boles thin to the widener of tracking turf, pylon by terrace of heeded instrument! If the tree-standing for wire is the pull of cantileaf, what can indent its continuous ornament looping on power-line? The trees are resident by unavailing advantage, full technical sorrow lattices their derivative store of staying beside-hand a cloaked way below. Each wafer strut as actuator, soft spring between wing and store. Field follower across overhead pitch, into the straits which fertilise a neb of impasse, but where wire cups to its beak a lift of towers inciting local spine, so spike your green along. Forked untransformable at heel of branch, trees topped for their sail-at-root, they bare these iron masts whenever nothing can have happened to the great limb.

Penned to place browsing rubric at passover, a hangar of unmixed trees is to the very source so little absorbent of archaic refuels off line. The pylon position anterior to ground raiment they are the plantings beside. These graces rest from detail, a culvert where timber narrows from indigenous refuge, crossed by splint of site-renewal, but always beneath a mono-difference which is for cable the single swoop other, inelastic divergence along towers. The trees perform the alterity at a remove which decreases into their own, derivatives at an unmoving dispersal. A current which tilts but levels out effect shorn upright at each organic corner. Overhang (below) steers to an angle shady with branched case of the relay, delicate tips hardly shamble a temple of greenest cages on stake-by. Or seed initiative to the more consultant rigidity, parapet of a tree's outwired profile.

Confession to gantry is pure-pining for a fabric of previous limb, cut to sidings of nonhuman repetition (stable remission), given a tower-split to land on. Meanwhile, the trees compare obedience to this graph of the open hearth, its free hollow is heath across them, with what remains of their own nape of verticals prised towards porous tier. Sigh for morphous readiness, precariously inactive by what discerns the infill. How easy the open is, cut commonly to infinite row! It coats the plantation's corridor with escape-stint primaries, attachable outward healing alarm in green.

Rising margin cocoons a planted oblivion, the landlight of surge fosters a dawning onto apron stake, conductors made nonspecular or no backing for tintless trees. Light can do nothing with this holster of woodland, keep it drawn to nurture only where it was outmarched. If denuded to a sentry of passage, still the pent tenantry of spending tracery like iron branch or root.

How trees stand ajar-remote at their reparation schedules. Sitedly gapped, no use-of-passage goes to unless it be their misassembly apart. Incompressible flow knows the studded circuitry of tree load. Detection of infill is raking the conduit, flash-overs of insulation are stroked transversely by the branches' own shield cable.

The tree like a cradle of wire has no pylon-pause for the elevation. These superstrings awake the wood cord, bake over it. Braced for the inexhaustions of line, insular cup these greener slots sip, shade slipped through needle. New wood transfixed by a peremptory earth's infused tower. Swathed forest interval roped aloof by the kilter of interruption.

If this, too, composes arenas of completion, the savings were too unwandering for there to be any linear invective against inclusion.

Wire sag falters no crossings, increases fibrous entreaty by way of its attrition not entering but swelling out shelter. Root means square error for non-linearity, cross-stalk, or drift with no output other than put biding the contraction below-mast. The hazard is trees pose no traditional housings, unhidden by brilliant conduction of own limiters. This secondary panning to pylon is unintervening, a leaf away from mutilated ground.

Seedling pine caught gridded onto relational scatter, lean lid for bare earth, fraught with the fundamental parcels, lesser infill, the siphons of burden. By-posted, assigned contrastive vitiation by a vital lifting of frames, and answering with the little purchase it is, continuable small rigidities of survival on receipt. That, with time on charge, the outspread is starker to join aside but patches for release the space of it during anchored tree-bed. Scouring rides of turf, the flow of pylon cleaning the woven. With stunting-yards below, perfectly alive slabs of nestless orisons, vested to a humility of the minimal stiffness of beginnings. Horizon's bole is pylons' drop platform, saddled increase in distance-to-cable at such half-anchored world-brakes below. Pines cutting low over the hill with no swing to their throw, fawning on bog-umber for outlying water, retying pylon-ember to attempt the strings of the sun.

: import of knot, insipid at the young high towers, forbidding no placidity against bleakness

: pylons kneel on the air, trees fold a co-striation only, dress to it their offerable hulk of surpassed result

: interior wiring transients, uplift for foundation in dense cohesionless leaf-coil

: any remission of pylon is real scene, the contrition of sealed by diverted green

2

Five Plantation Clumps Near Twopence Spring

Somehow I can't help flocking to plantations of sallow inquest. As if obeyed that resentful pool made sheeny by perforated rest. A net, not fully woven onto narrow earth, of nearer, sparser horizons for anywhere shelterable yet. Five courses at an arc of tentative verve, a counter-furniture between preventable barren grain.

Unclipped, wrapped shadows, the irregular huddle coating futurity is various ages of prop where you don't fall on arrival but aren't shielded by surround across such seriously enchanted plans. Though something is well on with awning over local stretch, feathers tailing in its guide-stick, an outyard of leafy arrows. Less than radiant cavity on the spot is its trees over it.

Coupled or cammed fluting, a porous belt stretches fenestration to enmesh ovals at canopy, beaches in wafer impenetrability. What blots into tree, stacks blind a particular clump, I now can't tell to be surprised not to be leaning into anything here—this woodland frequence broaches restive clips, commonly neglected cutout. Along these instilments beaten green we share an unresulting entry widely offered as if to non-partakers, though there are none. Where a through-hallway is openly scant it's no longer empty, but sent into sequels of reserve, nurture blankly observed in its liminal rigidity. From the dappled niche this side of it given, handling the focalities it is handing on, any unaccompanied horizon is brusquely kept at bay. Embayment from here will forage towards a more markable ring of what there is of it, too little to put down out there. Pre-fixed fingers at least know the fractions of reach, keep the landscape's waxy criblines stubby but cristate in the roads, rare rods once they seed. Trees abbreviate where they collar their rinds of origin, a debt so paled and unfrequented as not to be called for under these rates of cover, striking in aperture and outright arising.

Among simmering clumps something committal, the holding delay sorting into times of quickened hold, combing the honourable brittleness of what can beset occupancy here. Abrupt resumption upon stiff wave, no bridges between the resources. It cramps spools of light shining the axle out of fringe, close-grown now as spindles mown-to-light, these stores have seen midgreen through. A mould frittered in woodland jammed adjacent to empty pincers of the ploughed wold, a nothing-flaring which mists and stiffens the wanting to leap overhang. Unshadowable null difficult to caution, bright salves of dedicated breach. A nought of nature astounds nurture by these simple visitings, hounded to right range on behalf of each frontal of trees. What is to be sheltered is what draws, tacks before additions less continuable, with unstable arrest enters for bunch any remedial arising cranny.

A static pact with projection, no tame slumping at the dug-ins of circulation. Stations along the sweep into arc, often as not with the holding spell for sheltering dispute, to stop along the way, blocked into being on the way. To say of a clump that it gives with winding down any primary escape out of attached provision—attachment brokers the open for its unenshrining commons, but stowed for numinous standing at the open, entering it on behalf of any scrambled moment of the unbroken. Scraping the cyst onto its sticks of origin, the waving harmlessly ribbed enough for uplift. It stirs cohesive swirl, locally unfettered but toiled on a spiral of thinly rigorous attraction. The random fillable, litterable, whatever fidgets between the recently unexpelled.

The clumps pit our approach around middle-detours of a menial space, not so untidy a hurt over their own spits of arrival. And ration us to this abiding particle via their own captions: a life's force copes a life's resource over the fountainous-unsheltered. In distended community offers its no longer intricate knot, but the loose lances, weak stayings of its vertical shadow. If uprising was through the hollow of the knot, it is since an horizon's trace became not solely taut in the eye but furnished in slackness within the knotting itself. Held open by darting that spar of shelter between itself and its hold.

Unblown offered recorded, slightened at will, between the skinny re-entry bays of the wood. The intrusion of a breach into its own healing-space, a sill of reserve. So blunted upon own foreclosure, it stains the gift of this place, patrolling the rounds of true burden beyond offer. If leaves drop, they pelt shelter, over frames or from branched frames—this is for reelings-in of a sea of wheat or rape. Not out-given, but given upon scarcity, serving what little of it the plenitude of a within always unenterably devolved at the swelling pores of a without.

A green credit which ventilates one spate of deprivation from another, with another, a secondary fall-back upon unheaped shelter as time grows the usual stickings over itself—that the promise couldn't so punctuate and circulate if it weren't jogged by primal forest, the instinct (not the vestige) of jutting into, an apex of having stood everywhere. Are these trees the non-liver, or a greater bowl, of this boundless waste?

From initial pressings onto site, these clumps are unlike arena, but, pared to angles of association, become a circulation of non-auxiliars, adaptations to a broken proximity, which breaks through the neutrality of distances not given to co-incision at such stabbings. A circulation which is then the fossil exactitude of riven shelter, here degreened to a living infrequency, but taller keeping with glades not yet renewable. Already rigidly dealt to place.

Serial relations clump contra acceleration, compassion is the trees' mutant stiffnesses not immediately for an unloaded flow of time, but a derivation which endures its tug round local compression, irregular sanctions, perfect stanchings in little relief.

Not a circulation of one thing (which would be an uncompletable) but a cutting (copse) which pricks into partiality of ground at the slightest vertical patience. Shelterable outposts where arcs by analogy with surround overstep the one, but bending to traps of enactment enfold what as trees doesn't stoop. A trip to plurality is the stilt-share of attachment's inbush. These gift-storms blow back to the *lien* of the alien, in lieu of a ground-lift which is scarce piercing of ground-target, entrussment of untyings of horizon winding the same residing. A vertical leanness-to-stop startles the gap onto ascent as byway. Nesting rents, woven into an embrasure of the gap, whose embouchure is pursed along an horizon of scarcity. Calm, unassistant, but not lack-making, screening inwards towards the lining these smaller obstinations are open upon. The gap is untouched, unfilled but fed, occupied to a slenderer drift between fortified irregulars of trust.

: to cliff green shell in pocket raisings-forth

: tying in what chides of the nest, no splinter of assent flies away from bush

: a world overdue is despised for clump, a guest in debt to scarce foliage, but even so

3

Palefield Coppice

Without quelling horizon on the outsill its blots are from there to reverting coppice, a long strip's bright harrow is incursion to place left uncut at the bine, radiance visits capped. A holding of border-position at a greenstrap which has swung for short across the amount of throw: as a blocked grid will do to shine needed what is abeyance in it, at most semi-fruitful that it arrived—into a telling of horizon.

A wilderness unangled by its precise print of damages, now in measure of green ceiling. Here, banked supportively at the turn from edge, not haunting the fore of us by any keener function. A wainscot not wide enough to concert a world, but offering its face behind a direction where partition steers in case of prior lengths. A stock skirts horizon where there is no store of it.

I stand at the corner of good narrowing, the woods as they near, or stiff light to be shorn. Not literal converging unless vacant entrustment marks a green vein pass along the bisection. I hedge outside rich composition, content how a tree-tightness rights itself off the shore of interruption, segments my approach to it bruising much the less movable. Not a transplant of scattered centrals, but an unscattering of singular load on behalf of.

A target for saving stem, wood in this undetachable bin, settled splint at chapter. Narrative doesn't continue, won't leap over until back-arched far as remissible, then let this repose in place of horizon transmit offence. Scarcely a skipped emendation which is not towards the bereft into link.

Something quickgrowth printed in tartness, new sheen to undertravel the daylight bower with a snare which sprints its revetment of seal. Already spears shuck-off the light's defence, standing mildly outside like larches of locally sped texture.

Follows the bright, undeliverable path across trellis which deepens the overhang against mere threading way, these brushes know the spindle-selection of a trap on the turn. That we becalm, ulteriorly dearer than passage, the spare, compensatory space baited at a sphincter of our coming signal that searches closed. Feeling the filament which infests the rooting emptiness, the tremor of it fillable. No vehicle at this left for gift. Glistening to entrap the spin-cell, enchant the giftpost, to coil it round the standing slot which has it blemished extra-navigatory. The shallow of a shelter over it, lesser shadow for root, pressing by gift.

Brief striations of staying, reassemblage to a swirl of outspin whose distance isn't in place of, but a loop to green fixities radiantly before: an obstruct-scale requites lit rods which are bold slighting, on the way-to as abstention is grateful upon any thinner continuance. Bushed light is injected belt across a sequel leaner through light, the winter steerings.

Contiguous where plantation-level shoots up inner cornet, tapers out to corner aprons of waste union.

Shallow relocations, stopped by a stick of place blank to the ghost of prior furrow, unjointed post as if at a flesh omission of grateful hold, we are walking for shelter instead of the additions of it. Blind bones go coned with the shrivens of a certainty of interval, whose latch haunts far towards further onlock.

A detonation of striped, reclothed light is no horizon to be offered at empty sight, more a deferred relic of future limit, distances which cannot lie open but which must be prematurely sown. This is the offer covering forwards, slight sites of it don't grow further toward. Fettered by intimacy, lesser in place to be a cell like distance, and mark the fore-spoil of true preliminary spindles on behalf of. Green refreshment at its slackening net emitting the arrest.

We have never spent less on entries than at this wood-corner. Deepest near whose pore will sponge dry, dust it with what wants to be imposition, ambition of penurious mesh. According it that scrape of entrapment within the fresh scurf of an ingle, aligned on abeyance if it will fire its bright rind from cheaphatch of corner.

Scarcity crossed by collective shells of infill, elastic in captive message assigning which hovel leaf is to be pinned at foundational push. The crush of green flakes capsulating, until the search between can be unreserved a moment, suspended as though all opened onto glowing gall: lesser fall, slow to ground, is quiet business about jacket.

Bands across the stakes, passing through is only this transversal, across thanking a detainment no radius but bars of the dedication it is, for nothing less will the pegs bring. Which skimps profile to become an interlude of primary hedge, not sliding ahead of implantation however it shrivels on the changes in dimension to itself, the spurn within green. Fields don't plough into this, but ply their tideless accelerations in its wake.

Dark woods for sure veering but no paring of the offer, not centering what the lithe connectives stub out against fossils of shelter. Local massing gone speculatively slender knows its slacks to the fill, but perplexes what slots circulate older leaks. New gaps divert brightness straight to the pulse which takes a tree aback: brilliant chasive cramp about its vocation.

Poplars on the flank align coevals of standards by mending moving line ahead of heavier ovals. Their winter shoulder to grow broader-lean upon the starveling print of place. Arrivable signs drawing to the vent—marks tensional consent, the valve is tree-crater familiar weather in the non-storm available.

Bulbed linens, your stillage is sapped tumult but billows to a mutual carding of leaf track branch, rakage devote the open. Or leaf-feathered in conjunction with salvage, restitutes the shut beginnings of offering and takes it across the bedding peel of subsident branches. But not islands of florescence: blocked corridors cross with horizon a diminishing light, shareable, snareable. They are its fill of scarce, blinding attachment, unfreeable spark darkened at any tube's seam which has all desertion to impair.

The spur of a tree is inclement unless allowed this seam finding increment, starving itself to front an horizon in bond to its series, a blunt nub radiates full across the blank havens which deny it a floor of assent. Spikes amid the issued shadow, stalking the open which all day loses fold on a percentage of life stricken to be granting so little hold by nurture.

Under a breeze loth to invent lances, leaves shave to their sheltering ransoms, linen of the trunk not choked but hooked. Lacking nothing better than to return the crooked to the hung: obstruction equip the throat of horizon, no other exception than lying across it.

A sifting of source lends brush, is horizon letting through the present unfurnishable edge, until this plantation is dressed for gift a long way outside its aided exposure: an unpent dusk no longer presses at its root. Hoardless once it besets a beckoning from outside, or quick-sets its hanging for the outside, which won't disdain a border this far back. Too near for a boundary local resistance might yet weave, but goaded with upright sticks to chequer the outer seclusion, offering-on not as if from open to open: trellis of attractable seizure, tincture scuttled at an horizon's defunct inset.

Sustain the ajar at a bar of terminal edge, to risk the abide of. Stiffened by expiation a green cage at a time, a breadth along the outpaced. Singularly attached line throws a spine which is moving-passage forever understocked.

The sender brings back this eager ghetto, elective huddle with all the spares of resplendence, spending the components of sky and prism in weakly encroaching trees. Whose piers stifle lift until vindication is distance crept in at the ramp, at local stop-height worn warm enough for dedication to reach a shore of the caught. Given that a stump does get horizon-rich, or attachment is to be mauled as far over radiant barrier as detains the one green sequel before.

This foreshortening, horizon furring over, is the gift of an open which can't get nearer than a stationary offer, which sores in its sift, enstaling the irradiance with horned shrift. It is when gift can be stumbling the offer, not, to be on behalf of, going ahead: it beacon-finishes or border-burdens the unmet horizon.

Towards that protruding particle, the black wood humping horizon watch for watch, the wood's hushes damped over it, within whose line our nearer, plantable trees draw elation from their lighter combs of shirr. But fording horizon with that overhang, all the coverts of it inland of the take.

Poles charred by each turning, heavy gates to such setting down, frames knit to a presentment: what they can owe towards offerable burden where they do not go. Attenuant dedication, it didn't ensump void, but drew these mappings of plug in log to a lesser wedge where it will be stored as poured, as a pin is circulation inclusively stunted, unflowing but open-drawn across the vertical dedication which scours for infill.

Horizon as pure gain above endlessness, the line of it immediately below what will be offered as a lessness which continues, not at a between-distance but connectedly pining at foreshortened obstinants: the tree-clump tight-spaced, embodying horizon like a pigment of its frame but conjecturing the redundancy of own particulars before a plenitude scarcity is best token to, scarcity less a mediation redrawn upon coppice than disabled in the taken-to, collapsed/entangled at sheer stick-drill behoving distance: scoring the landscape's hard-plaque with each taper alighting through it.

The tree and I sign off shelter between one feed-runnel and another, an open bell broken from funnel: there blockage is bowl-ended but lighter in the awning to be broadcast across shadow. Short shadow, so difficult to grade needy, wrapped out of exit, crouching below the currency of a universal it must glean, touching bad joint of the scarcity of it offerable.

: a pitch in the sky will be index to this rising inexposure, but ceiling proof is to flatten out the finite at its dressed, onward resting

: an arched hem gels to an instinct propped home, its swept gate to binding greens wrapped in senders

: taste the wind to see where its bedding mobs, studded by a solitude of dedications

4

Coronation Spinney

Some brow waiting over limit, a cease-fielding flat against because a wood would be paltry awning it. Impacted sack it was quested off horizontal rut, the plantation seedless enough for upcrop through major surround. Deliberately rafted on a spite of scope. Wherever the fields are unswathing to pursue to a remedial, as slighting does by transhaul across immediate waferish bulk.

A breadth of the floor's horizon bending into flange, a curtain of first firs in the glimpse. That a ground wave is broad scrape to everything sowing but at its broken rail there is serious coil. Trees sting to the breach. Relied in band, relaid in depth of tree pressing the cabled open.

Furrows roam in lobes. A furrow thunders by canopy, continuous to act with what season is simple off the intermittent spilt root. Co-secret along the heath long agrarian as were trees, their propping more stonily cropped.

The heath unpacked, fins of it achieve wheat or game-corn, or poor pasture floors it, usable at a dusting of feed not trodden underfoot. What is buried is retaken in desert, is earth inasmuch as thickly shaves the beds, onto it mill sockets of forest hoof. Indentation creep of a direct felling where grain precipitates boundary otherwise soothed in wheat-height, its shadowless induction.

Until a ripple of barrier breathes from the intake of edge, plying leaf through the floors, will stitch the coverless granules of the plain. A ruck at circuit splays before creep-plain but chafes with upseep, secretion early at a bound of openness jumped by root.

Doesn't bar the trailer fields but insulates them to strip as its own spinney skimps, takes bareness off grain at large onto intimate barren survival along a lime of overhanging: adherence no nearer to non-linear warren but whose bitter fruitage won't restalk according to strings of the corridor.

Are the trees anymore so obtaining they can pivot on the blockage, that the halting isn't to the fore of adhesion but abated at the dedication?

Furrow landstorms approach by stealth rising in the stilt, along an impoverished ridge of the wealth there is in appending sticks. Crusty proportions of one horizontal not quite brandishing another: brush-value inquires stir of the vertical.

That the harrow has chewed the roots off allows the plantation to fathom these stalks: asides from the food-window are spindly by proxy, pressed into nurture at an acquaintance against ingest. Steer forest for what anchoring it smears off promised span, a blain out of the working crust. Unprehensile in the loft it stakes to edge. The trees rolling up banisters pole for a cavity long levelled away by outfall in the grain. Recouped spoil following up shale until bole.

Stilled to a basin without stoop, brims until the edge rails at impingement, flush at what the poles infill. Cribbed from surface once the grain of it pools a ditch, wherever some skin reservoir defected to threshold. Knee-creep at throwings of wood, but no scooped braid yet: the fringe tapers from grains of the flat lips of earth. So much dust-ocean of passage, toward the sake of a tiny rap by trees on the hollow edge. Rising translucent, filaments give encrustation, a trench no deeper than the green skirt it flaps.

Are sparse aligning segments a resolute queue across the divisible? Its seam invokes lessening if the pincering apex installs defeat, with plight to fold outward a verge upward for the over-run. A redemption budding the natural array of contraction, a whole weave of intergrowth can pillage to the still of it.

If land at output, to be spared, will feed a protective crest along its ridge tremor, where tree despoil embrittles its sown trailing dyke. A wood alignment grazed smooth for rigid renewal like any untread.

A cubicle of leaf at the parting by bounds, whose cell pecks for invocation: where the lip of the open isn't breathing the disappearance but holds for relief in unpronouncing snare. Let it jam upright alive in plentiful middle of valve, stretch the field one tie-bit extra across pull of common pen.

Will this be stoma along a secondary sedge of fields whose plantation drought has long since relinquished the blame of a natural monotony? To grow sustenance about scarcity's lane of offering unhampered by outspread: the spurn in fruition quietens the gatherable.

Within the long corridors of the open a wood niche hollows the way, a line of trees freely in midst of margin by an exaction of arrest: the effigy leaning through the flow, follows but shows compressible counter-grain.

Until the journeying of the production lanes is re-violable in strict foreshortening, what gives blunt plug to shelter. The criterion of branch is to stump toward speculative cage empty by way of any other containment.

As the plaque of it might be perforable but in requiting that much stays unspread in hollow: what opens to is not remissive but transhesive of a tree of the withheld. Slightened to a coil of speculative barrier.

What will stay in the world consigns by ream of all that must sheet it over edge: trust to cover, or crust on behalf of collision, offers a film of arrest at the loosening bush.

The wreath subsides until rimful of itself. Landing on tree as a weal of flow to be offered for outside ledge: if local much diminished as non-exposure, peeling it offer out of the welter of mono-layer.

Not pines of tenure but what edge frays a weave from, the tassel of donation off votive deleteria. A wreath of waist-thin trees tending to focal blight, a rammed cell of invocation will serve as buttress around the indifferent convocation: the disparities they weave until studding the traces.

Choking earth to smoke the firings of trees, strips locally medial, radiantly slicing the impacted invocation: not between but how the interrupted bud swathed over the one raises a hood of dis-eruption from beneath the other.

The interstice is reluctant to divide except at this living erosion, pristine separates inspire an intimacy in ridge. If hoeing the earth into acceleration then vesting its grooves in safest breaking, sheerer capsular delay overtakes *into* the stifled harvest of trees.

Nature lives the glading to be stumped, slighter by niche of, the mash from dispersal plumped too harrowingly on: the flow of it survives by very little by siphoning a foliar likeness from scales. Taken in the shade of leaf but gathering horizonless shells from the sheaf.

Trans-facial the contractions go, to which horizon isn't distance but unthreadable implantation journeyed to the barrier's fluting, lightly stunned at duct. Stunt these liminal runs until trees are hardly bare, peel a stint and what flakes is a tumid printer of leaf.

These vestiges spend up the lessenings of absence, a stance into row keeps the socket dangerously stowed. Sensate retractions, a tripwork of obstructive locals for focal.

Local shutting reopens nature's shuttering rate, a prayer in time with the gate's low louvre across indented oscillation: that there is offering, riding the notch, a mark on nurture.

A fracture coming to within heaping a scarce world on its pleats, invocation from a stump of margin this far introduced out of the flatness, full decline of horizontal at such a staring keeping. Earth before its offering, a tree-dammed horizon coming towards it: already having reached across horizon to yoke this side of a ground upright.

Its infinite oscillation outside-at, to print the containment from withinside the openness. Gives blockage so patient of the tie to a footage of web. Trees as if not drawn from any vessel of earth but only now spiralled and impaled, never so protected before as impounded in an instantly loosened dead-end of ascent.

Detritus a string of core-vestige, vertical length appears from behind its own stack of dearth: the health in loss goes a little upward to its nexus of giving over, by a spontaneous barricade of giving onto. To assemble around a rim which for trees is work of poor impaction. Reduced to the unplentiful in accompaniment, where plantation-edge is open ditch but with this symbol finds nothing but roof: a plexi-latch of ramification thrown openly across the sign of the weave.

A block of it gloves to edge, matter in green to learn crater, by which there can be a from of invocation: protection under the pines of a dimension's disadvantage. Spears it at its spinning onto the filled, its gutter lightest foremost.

Some brittle glow at the slightness code, creasing by minutest ceasing-onward but not cancelling ahead of flow. A chancel that the interthinnings stick at row. Propped cloistral-continuous it stays where the ration closes.

A narrowly endowed wedge for capping a ground appears in trees of interlocked escapement, innovatory contiguity.

Capacity unpraised but bestows the any giving-on, capricious in nature until cap-hungry, hurtled to the skewer of reception. A scaling rule for the landscape patches, not deposits but piercing with dressed tips its middle lanes. A vertical tributary from major plant platforms along the flush.

These span-coiled distances contour a surround, how a harrow combs onto tree, the tree's beacon is slenderer furtherance than barrowing at the horizonal. A line stubbed has it aligning in grace of, at the forepace of its very extension. Where compassion of the finite is an impasse on behalf of the endless, snuffed by supplicatory bestowals of enough but quilted with edge at the most rounded fold.

Woodland although over-placed from any direction the harvest plain proposes puts that unverging horizontal before its own face: an armature of dedication a single edge thick. A fray of crossing, pleached against passage, open to the slightest unrevision in the springing of invocation.

If the woods leak stockage they congeal to so many beaks of shade, because this plantation of it has some rare trim to prey clotted, a towardness not of flow. Thin pillowing columns: trees now far from their original points of emaciation, their joints are splinters risen to coatage.

Colonies of spindles on end given in midst of non-abandonment, a swell of roof at the tip of inflicted tapering: shade enough for lintel but free of that bracketing. Plantation to a breadth of atonement which is roof hipped for eaves sewing mild in the fields.

Not to be rifled through, but since tiny propellants did translate openness this is shift put to narrow eye in the shade. Until it grows to dedication by way of a slightness having entered, partial tubule furring truly, given at the real of passage. Not more than a blunt throw through the dazzle of the ahead, a hit off quittance.

Jars the flanks of storage not to contain any fabric of falling through, scavenges glitter of passage by raking up an unfulfilled onward. At the no-crossing is the turn to invocation.

Little simulation of light other than the predicament of the kernel itself, harried to a close with so much sparing recapture in the rind. Surrounding leaf-frame with a garland of interruption: by which invocation assumes horizon at this nearer fill-in, the bundling extremity it is unfull of.

Invocation at cluster, no cast of it other than owing local storms onward. The string of wood-skin an axis between offerings, an axe-point of clearance until hemmed in on the thrash. The vertical dues of cut whose severed costs refuel upright.

Arises speculatively static the moment there is a hitch in the landscape's distribution of earth by earth: now a retribution of the trees' prayer by dearth: completions by offering are not sites of repletion.

Ramific shards, amiss in sanctuary except where branches amass-through without being the leaner to, to their tips of leaving it to.

Abrading piny flatwoods they ache upspin, a bud of the vertical in blind-ended tube. Ascribe shelter on the outside of the probe.

Trees, despite losing leaves, seclude nature until it can be shocked up again, because they mow so slowly, right into the drag. Nourishment by scarce matchings of flow without any full flaring of the incidents in residue, the quietest slam into unencinct margin. Toward that pervious binding which grants a temperate fixity to passage receipts.

A counter of forest lingers on our exact sprawl of doing without, how we stake it empty-banded to horizon instead of furrowing it down to cavity in branch. Like an unblinded knot but a tether ill-gathering unless what an horizon enhances is as least before liminary load. Rinding the borders does scrunch at the oval of offering.

Trees again of their least consultation, pressed to have resulted in the stood, where for a season of the full horizon we didn't step through them. Weakness staying its edge (until invocation) within the collision-joints of the mediate.

This 'maximum of strata' in slight of its own retaining, held over any body of leaf crossing by way of gift. It makes a sender of the means we have to stay, a spender along leaf in grasp of declining sift. A choke-pore, brittle as root, around the flaking pull of the store. So did pulse make sacrifice to its filter. This scramble of detention is at the fate of it offering.

: an original withering upon keepment of sallow ties of edge

: to bring collision of the sacred into shelter of some faceable mixed fixity

: incipient rate of plenitude, travelling for the green arrest of the motif of it

: a bole surviving prestige of the vertical, spilling it over prop

5

Wotton Hill Clump

The hill's pennant at us, a crepance upon standing strikes up crest, but pinched to the foot of the wave: of the preservation locked seed flags away, spends the link in rarity of summons. I saw knots beat in the skimping-bout of trees at greeting.

It bathes in stroke of light kept thin to be notified, knit would all bounds be no longer buried below, stealing scale over up ward mesh. A shoetree arches a clipped leap from the hill, trees when they fill no harm of elongation beyond dome.

A radiant clump easily by spoke, not woken to its high chair, remains of the trees sleep from it steep upright. Tipped from a shaft of greeting, not torn where not taken down, its fold is the hill steady at poll, its swivel the beaten-off of compact skies.

Pocket of circle on hills' roots upon a trestle incurred where frame is all pleat: tall waving from a surround to an adrift sent weakly shut onto sky, in clasp of the impossibly smaller scale. Its inclusive island so late to be in tree.

Stretch sparse hulk of a next repose not yet adjacent, sheer patch into a tributary of sky, once greeted minutely grafted. Not branching but cracking into main simplicity, the fins and brushes of heavier-than-bare.

Composed around the straits of minimal hem in place of the open, the open put to defrayed butt onto origin, leading the die-backs which are the blunts direct. The bell-top of a tree-wave which coexists in that cell.

This oval cell of summary, by the slight of its own dimension left high out. Flexless flag if the pines (out late) are stuck to where their bend into greeting originates.

Air-friction weathers this waiting for greeting which has still to anticipate a throw of root, the ligature of a least-walk for trees.

That it's a sea of fire in the heavens we justly site tree to patch, a bay of air round a pool of trees, fiery abounding, dry bounding on a pillar of root, a glow which cones and arcs the hanger

The never quite tinted attention of a tree, we follow its pallor into the heavens, on the peeled welt of chief buttresses of greeting. The split of cover on a piece of ascent, staying borrowed in the height gone given guide.

Reeling exile around its few poles of home (stole over the hill's undistress), not an axle but a mast angled in no fleeing from greeting, stripping fuel to prick the air by which it calls, full to thinnest stick. The trees wave all that an overstress by which it can be less.

A tree-standard weather-chewed to breed enactment, a plain shadow maimed gives the clue that reception is a release no longer naming the sky for dispersion.

This clump a stance of erasure raised to a circum, a least-closed greeting by particles banded in smallness handed over the interval, a least without interval. No clump merges with cocoon, its yoking is subtracted but vertical to incite witness, a mat diminished as it avails, finished in the outbed it entails.

The split is swiftly not enough until the trees' way is to silt it apart, what they are with themselves, the gaps in grapples of huddled circuit split to be enough thread through the fit.

Sending for stone rings pauses before a rack of nil desertion, walks to its bed through a tree on a course now less than the force it tends. Mild spitted steeps in a greeting which doesn't *sweep* the sky.

Slopes of wall (a stoop for trees to be allowed the broaching) in a ring where each grain's pin falls into a stop of up (of which there is an up).

No rubble at this outfetch which isn't also wall and rim before soaring. In a leaf-hide of hill, stubs the hub line of a wall. At a rubbish star of woodland induced to a single cell of the cowl.

Pine resets dapple for impaired repletion of the outcall. Full cell that fall is spun, not just done to earth but a sill of dearth, its crustal beacon minimal silt: which bids internal sift be graded for all such foregoings of sky that will stretch greeting.

Chided by a cellular-scant working out of a complete circuit of sky unsated not to be beckoning, rod-border about unspiralling bed. Immediate cascade of climb from ground at the attribute nest is a destitution near enough for the distribution.

The vertical strings of its shadow won't rest until what is greeted sinks and prints the steep bars of reception. A wood gone clean through skyline, no sharper than lift as held, its telling-up inside cleat of smallness.

The branch as thread-body at the foot of its haul, gift of hold barely spun: that it stow there those few offwindings a spool has already begun to come in.

To walk into a scut of forest chased onto air by knot, to walk round the knot based on the eyelet of a tie. Packed at root, this unwrapping is a blow to the hill, even further to throw-away than routed at site. Scant jamming but enough rise for the holes of attachment.

A tuft's spurt upon hill is setdown, is hill hurt to an empty blade by leapings to a rejoinder without remainder. Soaked pines have always been blanching at the hod, but this is a carrying sky when opposed, novitiate to green interstitials of the burden.

Tall with stases in a silo of crosses, sown by no one ensign that clips that cradle except where one thinness beckons another. A lateral altitude whose seat of trees is hipped sights and stopped limbs.

The masts of one attachment to the world: though reversionary to height they mark it downward, oppressed to clump, entreat bruise not to cease but rise until trees creel the air, rest in a nonelement to which the little can be added their simple of repose among it. A few pinnings go steep in upon the hill's go-hold of greeting.

The same at very high advice, the seam in a sky of correction chosen to be safe stage from. Trees keenly to the smitten of themselves. Period rings of the stark, its clear wave over banking whose outlines concede enabling, the deprivation but of one thing over all.

Weather of a fiercely steered, each wind-example leads out spine round the fixed givenness, at a point where distortion resorts to limb. Staking out a rick of forms through which the sky is its own envelope of similitude, amplitude on a pontoon of puncture and tincture.

These jams of dedication no lower to ground, a hill is no further itinerant but tenant of the errant, its flag up in stops. Endings to the thing cause conversion of range: no body's root throws out a bed without the leap to lie on, whose bed sticks to the sky. Or clump it as a bed in less: sticks toward sky in the gift.

Trees must invite the source, such borders as they have a rip to reduce to called to close score. The innocent home will bellow at that clamp of trees costing a rising diminishment.

As one uncropped stunting across the deposing, if not a harvest of hill then a ratio of pick-offs doing land-feature, stilting to the will of it: their ungappings henceforward in a grown sky.

Tempering the margins which drop from trees, rolling in tetherable rims down the hill where projection alone is cradle, seeking out a thin branch of sky. No pan of surround nearer than these outspun contractions, risk of greeting in so rigidly summoning it.

Not matter of good-tie in furtive espousing, on a ridge of exile the descent is through a lack of spurn, woods have this beginning in their infirmities when two or three are masts of bestrewal.

It put rows in the no, a ridge would be shallow test without these stalks ajar in sky, jammed in their holes of attachment.

Late in woodland scenery, through scarcity toward the outer host of taper. Where you would expect its salient to be sharp greeting upon thin from the wealth of onset. Serrate better and no eye hurts from within green cynosure it lashes to sky. Deletion parks in the upper air, no glaze of trees in that radiant eye that is not a cystful.

Leaves trivial were they not so pressed, not feeding sky but lancing it for the crush-effect of steep token. They stipulate raising pine to a needle of cluster, for fear the hill might leaven out on empty squall.

Tethered-out from the flinch, it doesn't pave the hill's bowl, an upturned holster of smoke raises a tree's platen with which to serve to greet the thing.

On a hill a weakening evergreen fined steadily to clump, deliverance the epicentre of these small backs.

Some fragment of passage over all redeems tiny shake inside the shuttle: supply it clump's outer gift skyward from a furniture of parched interior weave. That sky and hill will filter the relation through this pitch of scarf: almost nothing of the enough were not a cell of stretch to stitch itself to branch.

A knot moots a hill as the foot of a tree: to quarry shade across enough greeting for it to be a link flying with pockets of compaction. An unfull light joining quota to outer, where a green-steeple grim of the reach is seating a sky in retreat of.

Speculation starved of offer, as thin in clasp as greeting it awaits a finger roundly treed in paring. No granulation toward eventual food except in those obstructions claiming their skyvent got thinly no looser, the planted grain along an horizon's unvisited edge.

Frantic before protective, a spillage on the upturn of sky once a cycle of openness can be pinned apart on the hill.

The clump heaps spare, ensures its ensigns of the under-renewable, no rebuttal which is not scarce welling of the hump itself: depleting to ensue a seating at incident of greeting.

The curvature stoops exterior, thin in the wilderness of vehicle, its hooding *through* sky. Specious in a sky's taking but givenness of canopy to its height fingers a clump's stake overtaken. A moat of the hill pilled proper to outreach where *contemplatio* retracts to the tree-mote of it: before socket such ditching in sky! A string of dust confesses in the eye, circlet rings behind circuit: knolling a bead in the sight but from the foot of unstriding it through nine beams: that tie-out is apprehensible at skies leancast off miniature hold.

: this nexus without rope apart from tired texture, twining a sky unjust to spires

: a taskless clump pounded in unseverance, hurt and parcel of an available

: a daily push on the sticks of praise, whose seams where knit do the chores of
the hill, spare flight of husk above any raising of the signal ground

1999–2001

Topographic Note

Turf Hill, once described as a "totally unjustifiable plantation" and now much reduced, lies near the northeast perambulation (boundary) of the New Forest where an east-west line of pylons pierces what is strictly the chin of Millersford Plantation.

The miscellaneous clumps, elongated or oblique, near *Twopence Spring* are also near Owlpen Manor in Gloucestershire. One clump is incidental enough not to appear on the map except as a reservoir.

Palefield Coppice lies to the north of Old Manor Farm, Haseley, in Warwickshire, and approximates to an inverted T with a footpath passing through the stem of the upright.

Coronation Spinney (though based more exactly on the adjacent Sixteen Acre Wood) is also in Warwickshire among the outlying woods of Berkswell Hall. Not in fact surrounded by wheat prairies but with fields large enough to offer that sense of open grain, except where some nondescript grassland survives.

Wotton Hill Clump, a nineteenth-century commemorative walled knot of pines now reduced to nine surviving trees, is beside the Cotswold Way where it descends from Westridge to Wotton-under-Edge.

At Wall with the Approach of Trees 2007

The openness at stake . . . is essentially the openness to a closedness, and whoever looks in the open sees only a closing . . .

Giorgio Agamben

The green cross growing in a wood
Close by old Eden's crumbling wall.

Edwin Muir

Non point la fôret ni la grève, chaque jour
Le site de ma promenade est un mur

Paul Claudel

The icon is always a wall that confronts . . . that can't be seen from the back.

Rowan Williams

nous ne pouvons plus passer dans une plaine sans mur

André du Bouchet

Je ne traverse pas le mur. Le mur me perce

Eugène Guillevic

1

(Approach)

Such large relays of forest seasoned to an impermeability of wall. Mortal wall wooded to houses of calling for uncrossing branch. What opens in the spate of the open lengthens the trees' advance to wall.

Trees not in tall barrier but surge a seizure of arrival, so far as wall crouches beyond profile. If margin wants this near, admit trees to shadow a wall in their lee which they are the first approach not to pass through. Bordered unseverable shoot only apparently shut-to.

A ratio of translucent transmission now needy enough to sow thickedge refreshing late classes of rapid approach. Not defence anchoring but wall quickening. Wall-seeking is significant greeter in mainline tree.

Less sheer attachment by tree than a proxy ribbon in the van tautening horizon by the thin of its recession, presses headlong with stunt what otherwise etiolates samewise empty offering. Transgeneric pocket grows patient with horizonal jacket.

Shorn linear stretch, of trees per rib of tree, nurslings given to interminable miniature cope whose resistance they care for, shrinks in edge for sheer co-invisibility of horizons not crossing it.

Given that wall compliance is tenderly derived as a pulse laid over it by wringing branch, thinning the proportion there is in liminal flow of approach.

Trees aren't propped by wall but shelter at a farther nearside (approach not being across) becoming its trans-stayings. In glade of, not passing through: a dis-locket hangs from the blunt open twist of socket-ahead, woods stretch with limitrophic neck.

Prick out towards obstruction the grudge of the horizontal. Narrowest unsupported verticalisation will run up wall rather than fold the flattened litter across.

Never stilled flickering of wall, no grain other than clothing in edge how a filter has terse bark: no granulations cross with such.

Approach of varied storeys in non-native trees not pinched or bunched before wall, but relaying the non-progression as a new asymmetry of hinterland, on this uncraning side of.

Wall not built over burden but as the trees implant full loads alongside: with any unbroken advance so featureless they snap foliar to disinvest, a re-scarcity equips growing ever stiller of endless approach's least end.

Forest-side suckles against bareness-to-come direct in the path of an eye-wall. A shower of needles might swell to blind awning these stilts of naked acceleration, but can only entail penetrable glitter on the palpable lids of obstruction.

Striations along the walls of land lineate approaching tree. Trees speak their upright almost from the face of this rebuff. There is so little tree/wall apposition, only the carrying into call of important ranges of the impossibility.

Slaked green walling not how trees plant blunt, but how sharp-before they are to be stayed from, by means of this approach. Nothing was shut in but the goal gets stopped out at its pure given.

A least spurious combination of them eases at this broad ramp stretching a shelterable of not piercing through: prevention is portion segmenting shade instead of compelling ride among unfallen trees. Would fallen trees ever break this current towards wall?—no, given their symptomatic uncontaining stall on approaching.

Where tree fall reveals pit or mound, approach moves to the sudden uprighting of floor which is wall-ascendant.

Wall-to-field margin a second time once trees remind origin of arbitrary edge at any several approach times its blockade: not a version of re-enclosure but offering field its begotten butt.

A wood stood-to, dividing in line despite the gentle pledges of its edge: a baffle calls indication out to the bar-insistence of approach. Not contractile, but a pause across the whole distance perfectly expanding, impairs by wall what is no length in thrall to deferral.

A tree turns where its stasis has ridden the outside-of along symbiotic wall guarding no other lair: deep-runnelled paradestination travels in gnarled trunk out towards this slight counter-rink committing midst to the cramp of immediate edge.

Rather than plant barrier, derive a wall upon the tail of openness, the whip-turn is its divergencies pulling to vertical spoil any sleek levellings of infinity. Root-like in blanked-out nearness to the difference there is in impediment.

Where leaves at tip curling to hem flick off a ratio of palisade/non-palisade, hang attachments out along neo-obstruction towards proto-release. If a wall of this diminishes domain it is all re-liminary to the defences trees aspire to approaching a spike of stop.

There is no trapped tree in the approach: cleaning forest edge of any closural scatter calls to open bound, layable wrap walling on interminable layerables of cross-over surface.

The wall bounces off, rebonds at greater distance than you would ever cross through. The outer side reduces to a counter-grain of unreadable face more motile than any passage that doesn't first invoke the spares of interruption.

Little absorption among tree-flows where approach is keen to appear at wall. The likelihood of wall is heterogeneous once a parsimony of hindrance can be satisfied along the trees' infirm outing of edge. This entire fresh fringe of woods is already broken (spoken for) in arch by what it doesn't lean across.

If trees surmounted wall they would offer its outer side the pure liminality of their not crossing. A call less pure than its further vocal patience.

Fleshly seamed-against the trees came boarding the earth as if along horizoned rails they couldn't possibly abound, until inferior to itself in flange the world derives deflection-yield upon the spate of a tendril tucked freshly.

If the trees have stopped at what is slight by wall it's since they wouldn't trespass a bulking which way they flex. Struck ahead takes projectives back to obstruction, revision is greened off collision: this side of how stilled is the division from deprivation.

Minor browsing on the inlay pace of likelihood once trees were siding with the more condensive linings than any moving surface is safely what its skin is. Trees not arrested before wall but copiously undertransparent.

No-fault trunk width but an adhering uncertainty in the approach intervals, unhollows of extremity abiding its call abrading from. Opens forest wall upon portions of delayer flow.

Invokingly a species horizon's distance sped to wall, the trees broach an outside they won't have touched simply enough through their openings.

Trees still approaching with every sign of wall shade into call by way of lyrically observing the impediment: not perimeter but the fipple ridge blowing at baulk.

How liable is world-edge unless it can also suffer trip-out along whichever surface retracts ahead of surface and then dares counterphase at the rimming of trapped grain, stunned beneath a screen of poles in respite?

Prevents migration through the wall but invents transfer (analogy) along the wall. A wall that merely bids for obstruction, doesn't block itself out of the approaching branch-play.

A wall towards the universe more lessenably still than trees growing their openings of approach. Which fills with seam the shuttlings of surface, weak in local exploration of the stopping places but widest splay at the halt.

Large onlays of forest seasoned to an impermeability: trees reach so far away in the ahead sheerly on-wall on behalf of.

Unafflicted attenuation gives in wall a coming open of trees: a green powder broods edge of use in recapture studies of dispersal savour.

Nothing disappears across what offers out-of because that needy, hardly sustainable, micro-barrier shows up in excess shelter of the trees' sleet of approach. Trees poach for the shelterable tide of no particular place's horizontal crease.

A body of trees doesn't partition but abuts, across the walling lap of territories. Not to perform mere tree-reproval work but walk out in the strong world-altering delimits of tree.

Relief not from a fixed, but with a met wall: how surfaces cater in grain sets to a critically dense now of trees arriving, all that complexity fork going no further than additional branch.

Existing the noise of a locality in replete defeat, wall as local as the regioning gives out. Liability of surfaces sparring a way, with all the boundary spears of this moveable earth.

Wide notice they are not advancing, inadvertency of approach enfilades horizon, dipped shelter not flinching at abyssal protection.

A solid walk of firs diverts interminably, until to be called over is to vanish alongside. Along the one ribbon of invocation invisible but for wall.

A wall too deeply sheltered by the approach of trees to glimmer with interstices, stands blind where what proffers it not to pass calls out the projective apron of blockade.

The nearest trees sustain a poor in world moulded to a wordless of stones inanimate as wall, the cry on becall of. Not a wall of trees but trees giving leave to wall, almost a well of it for the vertical to clarify in, but it does not, it won't trans-incur.

What is unchambered is partition of a turn towards wall, an entire expansion-lane of approach will echo topical invocation from these stops keying the air.

A shelter widening in spell of encumbrance, a run to deep stalling, so that approach is most motional in its discontinuation, halting in the advance of itself.

As trees came in they rejoin a thicket to world finishing, an earth only slenderly itself but shapely interruptive along a time stocky until edge: clean lip calling off these moving vertical tapers. A this-side on half its face for the outcome of all terms of the call.

Trees attain approach in as much a damage initiation, they prod pause at linear root to find the wound ails a wall, calling edgily from nulled branch. To staff a full-width tree as deep as approach allows.

Their universality over bare fields will never walk the wall. These trees in block are several stages further down their ousted throw, not even heaping the several jammings-open of the call.

Blind-stooling an incurve of ground, a coat recovering its lip. Forest approach consents transfer of voice between passage before wall.

2

(Shade)

Never so far rustle from tree watch, the wall is occupied in quietening the plantation's siege of being, recalls it into the shading of approach.

Wall-dispersed shadowings only begin to find the vertical in a wind which spreads the obstruction, to be seeded against trees in welcome.

How close into trees the smooth surfaces pan under, whose shadows play onto wall such wide innovations in rack, discontinuous passage patiently wrapped in single edge.

The open not just open but approached in silent, shade-giving accord with a walling-off. Dressed to overshadow wall or feed it well, until that supplied nakedness calls out a liminal foliage to stretch it short.

The weakest lane that can go through landscape, horizontal nodule which won't neighbour horizon until the stub of it is stood up at the delimit of tree-shades calling it out.

Trees shade out sky, what might have freed them from the barrier they support upon themselves if that wall hadn't unfurled a vertical trembling over partitions which re-owes all that heights dissolve in air.

A wall of travel that the types of shading are differential, impedance stays together for the offer of a contrary, no longer fixed in sheer (roaming) texture.

Differences of roots and foliage call out wall not to a depth of trees, but to the craning towards/turning from they are held over surface by.

As if roots take to the air for a high lattice stalled before a barrier not a pathway but a gap between shade and the vocation of shade.

Plantation at wall-to-reel boundary, a telling out of the deep shelter-midst of edge, however thinly wall holds it welcome. The wall to be turned at, not penetrated: the other of vertical attention.

Why do trees stop at wall, wall they are streaming full of when they run up to? They are its tributary—does this give them the obstacle-reversion of a global floodplain skimming over its infinite nearness to expulsion? The new intimacy they tip upright at this blind precipitation of site.

Or green foliage needles into wall litter, an elongation behind severed canopy sharp-speared enough for call.

A matrix of wall not reinforced by tree approach but simplified with the resurfaces of shade not crossing. Any apparent seepage inflects quite woodenly the verticals of it this side on. Only the call is another aside of wall by analogy.

So, reduced to their bare resistance, trees can't go naked up to an extremity: exactly what nurture is, foliage, intercepted shade before, indicates the increscence of wall.

Average local matter foliates, slices lengthways: prior to wall its shadings weren't fully a reach switched on. Approaches contusion in good respite of full foliage extinguished to shade for cutting edge.

Wall is low but opaquely so, even thinner fit will stand with the upright extreme outpost gazing from trees, but along the grain of a vocal crouch inside the showing of shadow.

Shades stand for the event called into the vents of light, this side of a pitch of vocables of prevention on behalf of.

Such life-stages of a margin as aren't internal but under boughs making out its only deposit. Trees not damaged but revised by the contra-flow of debris: irradiance coning the shade turns about until its glow is rewired off pointed wall. Can a rim be proofed by trees just one consistency before desert, before it leaps cover and unroofs a stemlike sky?

Trees a shawl but only at the blind point that any ending-resistance would end in addition (approach): earth is pledged by incoming, robbed of its blankness of order where trees have badged their shade to invisible stockade.

Arboreal behaviour crossing its range is wall-sought, filling the shadow-henge spotted linear under trees in flight. That trees creep to keeping it wall can be sheltered as the undissipated compression it is.

Under this peremptory shading a wall delivers a forest shore, fans out at the non-crossing what is to be exactly tapered to the surfing of call.

Heaving unshut against transit, to stay stripped by nothing other than a wall itself very needily shaded.

Shelter rebuffed but not for leaning across: exile also halts at the unplaced pitch of wall, only its trees prowed for shade press out the site.

This memory of a land's ultimate fast of impoverished over-hang was not to be raked over by particles accelerating the incoming plain. Earth's slighted ramp gathers to a shade because fervent granules do effect edges at, hunt in packs of piney grooves seeding a raised seam.

The trees hollow the movement but stay opaque to the vocational marks of a shade which isn't adhesion but call from the slightest, a transgeneric flank along obstruct.

Special chasings among racked edge but scours source close over when not without green roof. Present at a common border emits shade but won't replicate overhang.

We have eyes which see the wall. We only hinder sight by being seen out of the treeshade that reads us up an obstruction, pleads us to calling out the vertical extracted by wall.

Against supplanting a wall, the trees entreat what they don't cross, which will turn back along with them, grateful for the projectless requests of shade.

Trees are necessity to an abstaining wall, until installed to bring into close singular shadowable the end of reach.

Thrown sightless against the walls of earth, trees can only reblind us by beginning the limits within an eye of departure: their shutters blink, look to shadows of another linked opening-from. Shade is foliage in density of no traversal.

This side of a shade's outline not so much the wall's internal face as its most compact expression of distant watch. If the other side were to be imprinted like the offset of a voice, the call on this beckoning side with us wouldn't leap across to read it back.

A voice from the woods on the side that is left out to us, but under greenshade we have already crossed all that is left to us: sudden remote stationaries are now more provisional of the lips of edge than all the unmeetings of advance.

If you went to distribute its point of origin, you will have rebound it by the bent of a tree shading unleashed wall, by which the non-dispersal amounts to an offering: trees in highest ontological tension by extension to wall.

A wall untrapped by its course of shade, the trees unshed by their choice of desealant trap.

Unborrowed trees (not a furrow between them) but dipping at the wall, not even leafing the stalling over it.

To be unimprisoned here is to be giving cover its impeding due, calling surface to the presentments of curtailing its running through.

Shade-trees at a wall-length worldside resource, the whole of this face taken up by a larger offering scene in full tree.

Until isolates of errancy shade themselves, a pool of opening trains shadow along wall with a new intimacy: whose expectation is halted but the invocation is forwarding the deflection at over-marked, blankly fulfilled edge. Not at blanks but within filled barrier.

Call sheer of the cluster of shade-trees but in starkness once wall gives lip against empty crossing. The wall itself a supplicant now offered the tender refective twilight of a made mouth lacking a gate.

There can be no relentless forest clearing against a wall of horizon in quick shadow: the cloud in leaf shines outright its shelter flash in struck exposure to the enterlessness.

Rejointed in the coolness, a vertical grilled shading going so far with the very wall of the ahead.

Not embedded in root plugs but lowly rising up beneath the huge gauze of shadows feeding abruption this side-of. Having provoked a wall, trees will stay on to veil it from their own revisions.

That being-covered spires so lightly outward from non-being (the nakedness of not being stopped). Universal restitution is a width before a wall which can't be annunciation seeping over edge until a shield of trees dries out the brink.

That there is a rash to the cry is already something assuaged by broached tree-shadow fielded flush to wall. The tragedy of a future felling of earth lies close into these trees, bearing them a harsh edge they won't yet leave naked.

Approach makes bold to trees, like blowing the rails out of them, but so intimately slight they are sorted along non-autonomous default, newer detention learns its rim from the trims of shade.

Terminability of tall exit shadow at once cast untransparently otherwise, blocked shades edit its only translucence at the approach to wall. Any sheltered ground so falls due it sets out an arena of prevention in widest least partition of call.

3

(Inflections)

I

The openness of life bunches the moment we touch it with our own non-indifference deciding on vulnerability, the need to adapt as less than any overall economy of living on. From this lessening wells the possibility of a niche of dedication. That we don't wholly blend into a given commonality condenses to a precisely felt resistance, one we instantly recognise, but how is our cry toward this second gift to come through all the other crucially insistent givens? Do we then forgive ourselves horizon as a creative vertical, and not just the effect produced by an infinite horizontal within finitude? A vertical opening happens at a horizontal blocked, not a permutation of it but an opening-to or invocation. Not an infinite folded onto the finite, but an infinity for the finite, one that can be specifically invoked. To live the towardness of the finite as less than the economic (everything and nothing) sum of itself. Lessness reads off a numinous index that is any alterity set before. With no negotiable particles of being not already pre-burdened (pre-offered). We are weighed ontologically by compound fragments tacky with the sacral which cluster at what makes for horizon. So the need to avoid any nascent 'positivism' of never touching the dispersed—as if the other were not ontologically shareable. Scarcity (calling up wall) at the point of dedication is the fullness (in rarity) of a less-than which is at the same time offerably more-than, but remaining faithfully scarce, not more-than-offerable. Rarity greets the lesser, slighted by loss, both other (keener) than loss, and a loss openly of, not sheerly lost to itself. Our horizon is not so much an unknowable which ignores us as an incoming margin (wall) at the limits of our vulnerability. It is here God intersects with a placing of the world, not with that world's wider problematic creation alone. This 'local' horizon is like a membrane grown opaque through common (species specific) liability: creation must partake of creation, but always along the contusing (w)edge of itself. Not an edge of becoming so much as the scarcer ledge of already being given to be who it is becomes.

II

The imperfect mystery of origin, how a semi-chaotic creation compresses experience/ faith until the horizon of participation is more acute than ever. How gift erupts among all the ungiveables of world secretly or scarcely, without disrupting them in favour of some supervening symmetry of reception. That gift is so often interrupted or denied is a shadow symmetry, but one which has a radical poverty unable to rise to the brilliance of exemption. For in the how-ness of the world is its rarity of being taken to. Though the world isn't ours to offer, only by offering the whole of it as we trample among its givens/stalled retentions can we make any offering at all (what will immediately pin us, though not unshaded, to a margin). What would be held back as part of any negative reservation is that part of the obstruction/resistance of the world which desires in us to be offered as an incoherent whole to its 'local' margins; not according to its future but from within that difference which abrades us toward it, welling up from a weakness of God before world: but as the divine overwhelms again through the scarcity of call. These intimate perfusions of semi-chaos (precipitates of wall), or a remaining open to the exposure inherent in that exposure, so far as its horizon of active dedication is a further entering (registered as a sort of stasis) of the world's body as edge, suture, lip. A wall of which we never see the ends because it ranges wider than any dead-end obstruction: could only be this wall because both sides take the skimmings of us, skirts us like a current, a graining elongated by a counter-duration, never outside us, always further across, not so much dividing as combing and flaring. No crossing direct from one side to the other, even if, treeless, we had learnt indifferent approach from whichever uncaring side. The way knowing intimacy resists being blest by me: not a denial of me, but how the dedication of what I offer adheres along a world-grain in the poverty of being narrowly before such an unmediated neighbour of response (a this side onto). But will call, give way for midst of participation block by block.

III

How does a moment come to be absolute (subtlety of the absolute moment: Nietzsche) unless it is an offerable of the tree so subtitled, or what will always learn to find itself before a wall? Ungrounded without a groundless, but the poverty of not having the ground in ourselves, or even around us—it is how a poor in narrative detects a wall ahead of us, before which our cry elects the wall as the shaded, approached ground of our one scarce offer. Does our participation in finitude break up any horizon it might seem to have as we become by our turn extensions, profusions of the multiple? Perhaps not if our participation is blockaded by that very multiplicity in the guise of collision or obstruction, but then called from. The over-againstness of primordial gift can be restored to us at the source/impeded border of what remains active mystery stunning plural enigma once there is the simple purification of being drawn towards. The one that doesn't compete for its plurals but tilts the ontological plane. Scarcity isn't part of any divine economy but the 'point' (stab, stub, mark or wall) of any onslaught that might intrude the divine, and it is the mark divine plenitude makes on us as we share it amid all the other faces of limit, induration, sourcelessness. 'Scarcity' implies resistance within a world largely actual in its blank given-ness, but which grants us an allowance of a more exact directional, dedicational guise of gift. At the same time we are indicatively wounded by the partial indifference of the given as less than recognisable which so finely (narrowly) obstructs us toward. Does a sense of what is 'given' itself live out the naturalising absorption of self into world without remainder, but with a reminder to stay halted before the horizon's fallout of symbolic litter, before a niche or ledge of calling? Horizon not as interior demarcation but onwardly-charged limitation, the beckoning obstruction. How the finite waits on behalf of an infinite, nowhere infinitising itself. Horizon condenses this burden of anticipation as the hem of the local (where a universal prefers compression to selection). Less an intertwining or invagination than falling due on congested terms with. This side of the wall is itself an interruption of the nostalgia for enclosures: intimately across you, not narrowly around you. Walls of dedication roomlessly broad in their halting revisions calling out the changes of stop. Reducing plenitude to a scarcity of receipt reveals again a fullness at the given but shares entering the poverty of the given-to.

IV

Horizon that unconditional fold enveloping time, even as horizon as memory gets creased from within time, but not the same as what will swell contingently to edge, congesting but not buckling the domain, the asymmetry of a time-for. A finiteness of being resisted in order to impinge at all, an opaque crust on which we can't bed, but the call is able to move to the grain of it, a grain it intensifies just where the crust takes on burdens and conventions of a flange, a shelter-ratio the trees trip against, and so do shelter. It isn't the pure topology of the Moebius strip which is offerable but the tear in the strip of paper which incarnates it, and which must always undergo separation and contrary join if opposite surfaces are to collude in ideal depthlessness. Faith is the spontaneous scarcity of the finite to itself, in that scarcity beckons a counter-absence always in a state of a non-plenitude, what calls out the beforeness (horizon) of the prevention. How to think the 'join' in a Moebius strip as a concrete point of construction and reversal, not an ideal topological figure? The joint is a wall, a ligature by which two opposed surfaces jolt and hold apart just long enough to call out 'before' any violence of universal horizontal surface. If you proclaim somewhere less indifference of being, you will be met by the wall: it won't imprison you, it is ignorant of where you have come from, what you have met with and is never over your shoulder (yet knows what you have been held back by). It will divide offering from what resists it, not simply homing the resistance but offering the call from the impediment. Any wall as virtual as this is visible because open to how the trees nurture it at edge, only to discover its own slight but unsurpassable stiffening in what stays just in front of them for the call. So comes that fresh ripple between what can be experienced as offerable and what can't be experienced as given onward, except by waiting for asides of the wall. Pure singularity of event might not be sustainable across a world—burdens get coated onto and then gather and contuse in a sort of field brush, draw us towards horizons only too shut off without the gift of a scarcity in addition, ie how the trees get to what pauses before the slightness of an edge.

V

Any life-event which includes us is a freighted 'coming before', even though there is still the problem of how to adhere to the loading. Binding to a world's co-inhesion otherwise wallable anywhere, ie to be tied out at where it is horizon gives it a this side, this blocked site; but the cry of outside on this side becomes additionally blocked in, additively able to cry the fullness of what the wall expects. To finish at line as the linespread never does, its impediment turned ahead with assailing furniture, invisible to us but for the timed approach of trees. Inextricably open, enigmatically blunted drift, some draft of midst got upon edge, summons the blockades which unflatten earth, unfastens anticipatory seizures of call. Trees grow to the most unencroaching line they can openly imagine, but this sets off an uncrossable barrier just ahead of their chastened ramification. They don't room us, they wall us across world, adjoin us at the opaque sheerings of world. A wall on the far side of trees shuts nothing off, but is openness most carefully vulnerable in division: that there can approach a to-be-shaded for persistent obstructions of the finite, with a strong tapering of branch, conceding dedication at horizon. Call isn't encountered between approach and impasse, it goes unreservedly towards impasse, waits before, sharing in the essential curtailing which has spaces in transfer, its being before, beyond or shut out of, its folds and blind bridges: along its calling towards a ridge renewably crested by not over-riding. So far out clinging in trees sown by local desertions: the out-personed of us not passed on, what incubates the call.

4

(Horizon)

There are no separable wall-layers, only the endless diversions of trees laid to a reversal which prompts horizon.

Trees will image horizon by growing over their debris-flows until there is a frail wall to their dishevelment, the impedance echoing away from passage.

A wall that scarcely inscribes but awaits relineament, never isolated from the arching setbacks, bias of calling in popular trees.

In an open arena where woods find the micro-impediment spends them for intending horizon.

Though trees are not vessels the wall rolls an obverse off their tissue, though root flotation will push to horizon pitch it is not an elastic shore.

The wall has no free landing: any halt invoking edge bales out origin until horizon can make it across just where the trees don't assent to going off with the transverse.

A wall neither thin nor thick, a single trackless avenue as long as the intimate prevention within difference is, not crushed but hounded at the seam of rooted horizon itself. And then only as a compression on behalf of.

The sense in which an horizon doesn't exist is the density with which a wall does come to the surface for it, a tension of appointment at a deeply sheltered and dappled contusion of non-transition.

Rather than a failure mode of tree a node of the unsealable, a crest alteration in the pitch of tree: how branches set on low block assail the scale of horizon.

Barrier tone a formation the trees might zoom to, were they transformable throng at their halting. Dispersion otherwise so much in front of, so much on hand for, can't fit acrosswards at such turbulence.

The wall not hemming across but stitching within edge, what tree roots can't do for themselves. Edge isn't adhesion but prevention until the very point, exact foreshorted origin of call.

Wallable right along horizon, the burden of imprinting the difference, until trees are sent for in nurture of the shoulder of it. Arboresces a test projection so wall-like along the horizoning sediment.

Forests in the immediate vicinity of the wall show symptoms of exposure to its other side, a contaminated offering that couldn't have given voice to an arrival.

That wall might be a charged, denaturalised surface of horizon itself: we touch it as micro-erect, recalcitrantly local amid squat textures of prevention. Always premature with ribbony ridge but focal neighbour in the obstruction.

A walling this side-of disencloses the external from its glaze of exposure, reverts a call of passage to the other. The wall hybrid hasn't gone to source but approaches attenuation (of passage) to the tethered castings of horizon.

To approach a global parsimony of go-through but get walled openly at the edge of the world is as local as any marginal hindrance can read into voice that (branchable) graze on surface. Not addressing trees as small snag-units but for larger callings-off that grow horizon to a palpable impediment. Touch the stop-at, begin (call) any not continuing from: what ranges is what resources are arrestable.

Where mass has the concrete arboreal effect of making extensive an unslighting of impediment: vertical skin is virtual edge but the response is a keener horizon-face of wall.

Once blocked no remorse of eddying but the currency of voice offered. Away under trees which run the spares of arrest a surface far out to jutting earth: to be held to the outness of what is called halted, calls out, across a myriad untravelled.

These distances sharpened by neighbouring blockage never became lame: the trees throw away their props at this one lean edge.

Green baulking direct, any rim is only 'at' because sounding a skin, coverable barrier at pouting of voice, its compress of partings.

Receptive blockage going about its lessness in vocal height of the sounding stops of trees. Not rooted to a core of edge nothing so much covers as coming to the wall of it makes for voice of their hemming.

How woodland is carved to edge, not by cut but by shelterable lure of wall: sudden chaotic fixtures are the callable furnishings: not invisibilia but the vanishing-stints of horizon.

Generates abundant horizon off local blindings, how invocationally sufficient a scarcity it is that horizontals will be the parting of horizontals: trees play vertical host to the party-intrusions of wall.

Not snap at wall but stay from shock at horizon's kind of waiting so callably on the pediment of healed (pruned), unsealed (walled) root.

The surface comes out of its cave by treading up to rim, this ribbon of wall along which trees are a usable path to the unholed. If well in barrier mode, a free-walling relay in trees.

Find implicit density by wall and invoke perimeter rather than a yoke of it, so trees do stop at lure shall be their porches. Desist from onward contrition, offer it a nesting-blade for imposed edge instead of any clean creation all the way across the inert expansions of horizonless surface.

Surfaces induced in trees are apt to harbour a wall of endless face steeply ranged: rim more radically marginal than its overtopping in leaf. Fragile layer of wall roaming upright in woodlands was, in its right verticals, understood as no delayer of difference.

Exhibits healing by recognising wall just beyond green thickening, nurture on the far pledge of its range. Only a barrier's immoderate well can be that immediate before the translucent (no transit) greenhall of sending its pales for horizon.

Trees less like natural wall infill but act their revisions in post at a hindrance they are vertical enough to align the horizon's finding for.

Wall hidden ahead only at the trees' capacity here to know here, but isn't itself dwarfed by their greater world middles. This buffer may desire insult of filament along edge itself, long spiral grouping stubbornly at the missing midst of, keeping the ontological spares in bunched pieces.

A wall braced by hope just below the branch ceilings, an horizon is nesting in their being spurned along their way: and counter-traverses do make voice at ante-turn.

A way of wall in not stanching the beckoning on. Branch pattern answered by holding it as a pittance bidden, that trees will never abstain from the tall fare of horizon.

Trees serially in probables of somewhere else, unless chidden to approach the taunts of immersive edge along waves parted, invoked: wrinkled at a wall intending (not enacting) horizon.

Standing blocked and redundantly sheltered is more proximate to horizon days than the abyssal dawning of the open.

This no-opening attributing openness of being is flat impediment which the high trees' jammed punctuation cranes straight: they beam direct onto wall reflex the lean-to dedication of ribbed horizon.

Goes toward/combs forward whatever pinned standing we can: horizon won't attend unless the edging not crossing to it is overstocked, consoled in dense attrition.

Portionless horizon, intimately falls over anti-scape, impediment joins sides fleet of block, banishing this side-on any corresponding apparatus vanished heavily otherwise, approaches and trembles the obstruction a foliar earth of.

That the wall of their coming tethers trees on one side of the bad storm-plains they approached to no such crossing-with, but is ecstatically protected by them from the onset of horizon's alterior (outlip) weather.

Trees rarely the most guileless immobiles, all stasis has to go past them but not faster than they indent. To an observance of wall ahead they do shadow the untargeted, trenchantly startled of horizon.

A vertical distillation densely whenever that accretion is made thinnest to wall. Because you won't enter/traverse these trees they relieve the seam of horizon: whichever deprivation appeals with submission to call.

5

(Call)

The tree-beats are forward foliage, a stasis with all the growing time of invocation discerned beside this walling freestone.

Obtaining wall where trees hit on what vital lack no longer detains them from call. The wall isn't a barrier but an impediment of voice. No trees could stop before if they didn't stay for lip.

Once the wall is deep-edged with trees a far side impairs this side in everything but plurality of call. Not hollowness of projection, but every tree-spine in stranded-explicit lane of its calling.

Blockade models attribute a tree's striding to how the invocation goes charged: where there's no avalanche of resistance there can be little thwarted discharge of witness. What without crossing guides to the set-back ahead.

Trees don't remove before slighted wall, they stay aslope of it: isn't lowness not being the sequence of an opposite buttress but a stock of not crossing over which holds reserves in full calling out.

Trees save us from crashing through wall so we learn from the calling to stop full-before at the least of its bar: the calling-from is more placable than any scope of hindrance.

Go steep, trees, where roots are soaked by sideways blocked creep. Transmural blending reduces any cyclic bending by this separate side of, begins to call.

Distress steadied at a free-air exposure to wall, ie tree-based broad chasing. If blank transition reads ultra-blockade, it's rarely blind in its calling. Refusing to go over even the lows of a wall fuses voice with topographic lips of waiting, at least limit pronounced swell to edge.

No unclad genesis is inheritable, no unhindered abyss is callable, no dressed exterior without a bridging voice blocking affordance repeating the other side.

These trees can't waive wall once their approach is over surfaces made universal with earth-break, they winter in every direction from breezes of hard margin. So call pierces the oblique segment of denial.

Not to be entrusted with calling until that very deterrence encrusts a wall. Resistance made answerable by belonging to a banned face of the world, voiced by not crossing out all that is left over of an impossible traverse, what it can't yet be passage on behalf of.

This high remission protects wall which will be built out from the trees' overburden, that they call up to edge the induration of lip. Fault-tree of no releases outside the cry but easefully not any paralysis other than sure stretch along the proximations of wall.

Pause in approach flushes out the furrow in passaging, not to populate against wall or steal it from behind, but to be at its nearest surface, gradients stepped by a terracing made blind by invocation.

Irremediable wall assays limits to the reparable, as restitutional cry it must be borne up to within a farness of the outside's uncrossable fastness.

A shape raked blunt by some fundamental limitation, how local feature gave a start or twist to place: so far installing before itself stalled: what sets before it does, voice calls a setting-before.

Where voice, nomadic of the nearer side, can't tender any resonance of root resplendent in manifold prevention, has only the supplement of its own slack hold, there stoppingly calls out.

Openness sooner or later walled from itself may be the real comb of a world's margins, only on call can there be any shores of it before wall, our flesh exposed towards other sides at the nurture of never leaving the exhausted probe of this one.

Beside linear wall-stones which the trees convert to standing, call out vertical bluntness in a savour without gaps. Less deadwood than invocable stub of branch at the live wall.

One flank's asymmetry calling towards aversions of the other: a this-side-of pushes out one unimaginable pace beyond the trees' hesitation before wall. A wall won't defer its resolute opaqueness but doesn't confer any silence upon its single-sidedness.

No poverty of openness without a privation of the open, a shadowable of approach before which it can be no further open: great outer edge (infinite in local resistance) before which it cries.

Far seam into the precipitation of call not to invoke a rule of woods but inches up to a wall without any mark of a far side. Given that the wall wasn't recondite hindrance but the very search that offers conversion from crossing, given that voice is not at a loss but on a lip with which to take entrance from call.

Where the interruption is nurtured and can leave out in the world the prior vocation of call. Trees took on the burden of separations and are deflected by a wall of reparation, calling to be stayed for.

Ongoing shelter towards a bluff of horizon only ever locally non-centric, needing to be actively bled upright off surface until it can never again efface what the sheddings stop with lip.

Essential breach in surface can sheerly branch over, and so be ramified direct to hanging wall, the invocation beaching at a cliff-offence in voice.

Did the woods erect the walls? As continuous strip by which they would never be encompassed but so blocked-towards, trees let the walling be sheltered-at in their great gust of calling out the stop before asymmetric face of.

A turbulent wall ahead of trees will infer offering, their plight is not exposed. Origin will support failure when well-found at wall thinning to trees true enough for due impediment: dapple the prevention and concur the particles of call.

A larger wall had never been needed to invoke these late stages of a disenvelopment: a cornering (untransfer) of call but going straight on to invocation with all else subtracted at wall.

Exile also halts at the unplaced pitch of wall, only trees of it will give out the site: shelter is not rebuffed nor is it for leaning across instead of detaining beside an arc of call.

According to trees there is a wall. They summon us to open from the coalescence but don't provide distensions imitating passage. Remembering to voice from the poverty of excessive edge true scarcity of no trespass.

Immobile voyaging of the trees and other non-silences: the woods won't observe stasis, they allow a shielding point to open to interruption, the hindrance voicing in furthers.

Unlike a palisade in themselves but recognising the tapped extension of unslaked root, a wall of it the trees roof with no presence to break through. Any gap already available this side, perimeter will unravel itself to be a sheltered seam of invocation ruinously open-cast.

Surfaces can't literally crease for wall without a discontinuity of trees attending it. Calling the immeasurable by default body of wall, not summoning it beyond the holt of rodded invocation.

Trees that sign off all other inclusive spans before calling through the wall's stones. The baffle is weak flurry at a profusion before prevention, an inventory of no stalling this side. Any walling of trees will pack a scrupulous worldside of what remains of the keen outer sighs of cry.

There is a call-tree for each thread of the hindrance, direct entwisted edging for non-enclosure. Skim election of call off the current forest of deadtree? Not if invocation winds long and low as the wall itself.

Wall forever wrongline particulate stasis of sourcing the opening-to. Unpeopled invitations to voice-over at behest of inhuman dressing, or foliar addressing unclearable edge, not pressing to or even casting the shadow of edge over. Savour the incorrection that wall is, no erasure in the way of deadweight, but intensive clearance relays sorely at the domain of call.

A wall without any internal chamber, only the entirety of earth's surface brought to an additional impediment: can heap in line these butts of calling. Each living shoot contracted to a pleat not itself but followable call: trapped at edge growing non-negotiable fold.

The wall divides a side of call from its ubiquitous silents of refraction, invokes a boundary exhaustion before any other road of sidling up to a voice heavily broken out.

How sheltered, hard nurtured end on end by trees, porous only to the invocation: that wall will indurate a face of the abyss, only voicing beside the lidded eyes of.

Where locally stubbed far as dehorning increases taper, there a paucity of offering due die-back is never interruptible.

Nor is nature when downloading onto wall, but a border tree's zest for offering off the universal bower of finite edge, at a transfold of everything bar the call held back.

Stone Forest

2007

For Simon Lewty (and the postcard)

Note

The setting of these poems is the fossil forest above Lulworth Cove in Dorset, where hollow stone 'nests' or sockets are the calcified evidence of the algae that gathered around doomed tree trunks marooned in a saline swamp after a prehistoric rise in sea level (no tree trunks now remain on site). This is a scene I may have visited as a child, though I have no clear recollection of it, so the poetry represents an attempt to find an 'equivalence' for the place rather along the lines of Paul Nash who knew it well.

And how the absence of surviving trees severely marked in hollows by a site of apparent betrayal allows a certain renavigating of burden, a throwing towards, not simply a casting off. Here might be the phantasm of a broken finitude giving on to a scarce actuality no longer singled out as insular event; and so in its way more concrete than any pure possibility overtaking a trail of already surpassed particulars. Such particles as there are pass out like verticals which offer out of absence their own exactly scoured and rooted hollows.

1

We think of breccia above beaches, the leaching upright onto sunlight, and suddenly slow down on data mauled to stow a thriving at the swept-out trees.

Ruin pass root
to poach
files of tree
due ungulate
crater surface

This living down has swollen a pressing's crenulation, the reality-grid incites a slim niche of stature-tree become horizontal switch within brink.

Crater for a lapidary
upright nurses un-
tallnesses of surround:
bush-print of endpoint a
petrified flush
locally common

Blankly trees got reduced home unboned, but sit out in stones their vacuum clenching between nest-sands of tufa, allow it is a rubble focus petrifies the flare of trusting to strands of the disappearance.

Sockets don't storm
the net but set
a memory proof-print,
decreasing work
routed tree
into its fold

Abandoned kernel in tandem with its envelopment. Sub-tree gesture not as in hard bundling but comes by post-trunk raised handling.

Fidelity driven from place
granulates a park
armature, the fixed
powder of the riven

Host crumbled to rim is less a sky of dust than a husk transfer not defecting from speckle of socket. Group life does reduce to the centre of a tree once it co-abides such banked-up script of outwash within.

Which, when left
loaded, gives pure
buffer at a finished
diminished wait

A crater's shallow basking against strips of sea picks out in cooled magic how a tree enlightens what rock is reopening for it across braided seams of a socket in hollow.

Reduced contact
arena and thereby
come for grounds
of the eject-
ion's connector

Trees seemed loth to unload direct into socket and now scour its pots on both sides of the disappearance. Until the wake-up of loss is a vertical circling of horizon.

All the error paths
of creation in least

pool of a single
rampant backlog

Serving surface resistance from invert of cone where the well of surround masks this thorough hollow priming a core of reserve. That a socket resort cross-avenging time changes entering today's tree, explores reduced performance, or where the crater notched a belonging delay.

Devotion to site
rigid only in
subtracting from
living the action
its beheld note
of clinging the place

Cradled empty abandons to the offer across a non-empty ladle: pours on spoiled iteration the rut of petrified pocket, abstracted from fixation by a tree's memoried lip excessing the vacant. Reduced end-portion interfitting the sad apertures.

Trees to fit abroad
the communion-
clam. Primal trunk
defeat replete-en-
closed in stony
assemblance

2

The actual trees are not visible, instead there is surround of forest safer in the time run out of it, soundings of staying a loss in ring. Tree placement depleted in the barrowed coil, completed at the gathered hollow.

Face the end of void
socketful, a socket
bound to what the
empty tree commits

True disappearance is mainly incisive hold, around which support gathers, the join-on fossil of weak surround won't smother what the trees were holed-forth towards. Not at all slidable but on all sides of the focal follow a reception.

Socket-bite an
intergrace, trees
copy rock suffix
round their own peril

Where the source-tree is precise local injection, a covenant of provision. Which blocking solely gathered at implant is an entire next generation of platform renovation. Socket residue come upon botched hafting, the condition is allowed to set over low dismounts of vision in plug.

Open-the-sky supports
real vanished tree:
have compassion
on socket compression

The confluence trees train on our daily absence is enormous hub scraping us too. This clamp base gives it unstark according to disappearances, like the fidelity aura that holds to tallest baring, puddles an ultimate rotation.

Teeth of other
sign-lapses planted
in the calling socket

Sockets are from living branches long died into stub. After the tentative shade was ambushed the trees were reduced one whole hold, indelible fixed hush of a rock branding the truth of it. Spoil-trees behave like attractors offered filial rock-tautening. Though the conduction is socket, the flare of dying into place is never counter-traced, however shadeless the concretion, however wrapped the contraction.

Small ossified
delays (propagation)
and reduced rubble
score: aim socket
at target of
bluntest communion

Old branch-core imparts undisplaced erasure: to die in post and then surprise an enwrapment with pure socket projection. Basin-shaped that less than half its dimensions should spell orbital point out of post, the para-absent penetrative tree. Only there do sockets effectively hold the walls of life to this tree passing down a reducible size of belonging to the impact.

Believe in frontal
emptiness unrescinded,
startle its pod marine
pocky with horizon,
parent storm of
repulsed sea

How do I collapse a path within a tree? Crater-refer is buried outward to surface protesting the spine of time through each petrified standing of defeat on its trunk-exact.

Spate is entire
socket spending
tree layer: how
the non-displace-
ment (trunk)
does replace an
entering spot

Because trees were poorly dissolved, emptily embedded in the next relict generation of pitting for an earth at horizon. Not isolated in refugia, but horizoning by non-invasive extraction.

Laid out on
angles of breccia
in a nest
of instruments

ringed colonial
oral, mouth of
no re-siting but
disappearing off
an horizon's worth

3

No longer barrier trees but undistributed craters of a terrain modelling the settings of socket. A tree's depth of dependence produces local features in residue if its own sweeping aside devolves within them. Where trees are sucked upright straight through the onflow of time, the expression solidifies an unaccomplished stowage of horizon: shaped to receptive blankness by all the non-empty of a conceded attachment.

Trunk butt grown
stale to place
but trapped in
a crater of
embolden the mark

Kernel slide has induced tensile rock towards a progressive brittleness of surround. As in shared forest, set of all recessful roofs, tree attachment will parse a syntax of surrender with excess remainder: the seat of nest in its wake.

Cushion sideways any
craning beyond
desertion, but still
an ex-sertion upon
impenetrable rock

Though buffered in kernel it has queued its overwhelming to intimate socket. These aren't lost slave localities but shared locals beside a fruit in bowl of disappearance across the single locked footprint of absence. Any 'levelled' tree being in right measure of enjoined crease as banked blank issue of attachment.

Soft evaporates invited
a plane of weakness:
note the absence of matrix
other than mound,
trees in place
occurring to empty moulds

Exposed on a narrow bench in the cliffs, a fossil forest with algal burr bubbling a stockage, unblurred for it as were all such untenanted craters. Exacted multitudes of tree got tended at the solitary silicate pole. Not a hole bored through but (still lacking a nothing seeping) in avid blind fidelity to a stricken anchor of the vacant fortified: circumvented place is what crusts up the numinous narrowness of the plane.

Limestone with its small
tubes a paracrust
for banked projection
of remaining in tree

Tree body cedes its losing platform across a bowl acre reclusively hummocky in gathered range. Baskets of nest around the loss in post of how trees structured farewell by relegating the grain of their binding. What could be no marriage of trunk in earth became irreversibly new statutes of conjunct displacement, or a structure lengthened to hollowness where defeat selects adjacent (counter-innovative) pleats of completion.

Socket and tree-
crave, the drive
of horizon landward:
from deep nest
to referred mast

Less a replacement than the dimensions of absence belonging together, an after-layer attuned to the communal hollows of socket: so secondary concretions reform the site around whatever embedding (by losses) is outlying a retribution for that indwelling entirely found at fountain focusing disaster.

Layers of imitative
absence never
a lone crater,
they ruck up
a halo of
counter-partings

cradle staring at knoll
as rock of tree-throw,
root misses it but
seeds it a stone
of toppled bough

unwandering defeat
swells in situ
as such apposition
to erosion

mound-shapes over
quiet water though
all extremes in
the after-nape:
turbulent settling
into impacted face
with stoniest ring
for a tree's neck

4

Algae cushions sit that button-hole, as if blind puncture were put to the punches of how flushed-out trees point an undiffraction: pulled limbs are now paws in stone, clawlessly rasping at nest. Bone beds due vertical root-fealty pulverize hollows of shaft in accretive rock. Given such shallow knolls free of primordial root-jam, this contusion of absence is for priming sedimentary verticals and launching forward the stopped burrows of secondary support.

> Forest itself a string
> lacking interval, final
> incursion of the stone
> of belonging

Banked in mound, absence has no runway except in scarcity of scoured relief, an incubation pillow refers presence: how loss scooped at a cumulus of instrumentally yoked abandonments. Spongy dependence went rigid at this incorporate latter bowl, whose parafidelity won't quit defeat-treads retrapping the sieves of site.

> Mounds of record
> like a nascent super-
> structure ramp the
> desiderables of scarce
> counter-sift

Free salt swimmings sapped trunk and then baste in wrap mouths of ruinables cast onto enduring particulars of the non-negotiation. Sustain a stripping from site, deep structure calls for no strapping in the empty bowl. So forest, once fossilized, was never a gallery of conversion but a witness traversing preventions with all retention intact but disappeared.

Towers of spongiform
bone spin what vacates
in socket along the
zero held association

Tufa formation mounding unique to tree-crown like some modern jacket of the groin: this collar repeats from stock the hollow callus where a tree loses its own branch. The re-pleat snakes the leaves off forest cover with trans-offerable precision, or same ground blames for its badges of lesion. Not cemented to base but folded for inland edge of breach, the primal trunk insertion: hollow sump encombs a ground filling with horizon.

A petrifying spring
of forest absorption,
in saline paces go
integral inscriptors:
occupy strata out of
posts vertical with
reguiding the absence

Algae by the colonial unit courted by trunks soon to be grounded in brine. As secondary mould the rampart is out-clan. Defeat primaries took for their reproof any arisen subsidence sounding a razed rod-zone, what phantom spires sitefully elate. How the hollow sockets, sensing open bowl, conjugate the travelling root-sendings of perforate surround.

Algal in mat will
wind tree-fatings
through the suck
of wild tunnels

of attachment:
never hollow enough
socket if it lack
swirl of a place's

choppy festoons
of prehension

though root is barrier-
pierced tufa goes carrier-
hipped: lifts with
empty fore-cages
to an horizon
its overwhelming

5

Not a forest of volume stone but a fidelity concurrence abiding the spire of empty socket. Tie is simply an overbalanced tree, the bulb picket where you hear a steady stone in lithified current to openness. The root may float away leaving a socket ripe for pressing it, or a decompression of absence chambering the surface.

This is not tree-
famine but stonetree
shoulder, not defeated
process in fused re-
cess. The endpoint
a receptor's fine
hollow of dish, gath-
erer about desertion

The basic promise for removing kernel is to band in socket, as horizon of mutated (incorporate-collective) defeat. No ghost image of the absent (drowned) trunk other than a phantom grown pure inference in rock. Busy loops of counter-absence wherever the socket map was emptied onto extent.

A blunt bowl-reeded
transition, launching-
distance belonging
from defeated
in terms of

The queue for site-specific abandonment upon a placing is never empty: in the absence of correct kernel an unsifted surround erupts at calcified hold. The body's case was vacuous but the encasing is conductive surplus, so binding address will default to a referred-absent string of base.

Assignments don't strew
but rifle the material
landings of thrown
spaces, ample domain-
claims corkscrew the
topple span of
root zone

Empty socket now handles a re-future that there can be some exit covery: verifies a hyper-present on socket wall as remainder, secondary dependence being tougher in care than the vanished (lifted) core. Not a free space but an extra engrounded ligament, a root of weak attraction does the attrition better than vertical penetration.

A shallow crater rolls
open deep relief
attesting the taller
billow in its eye

Drowned in situ until the residual resident crowns out around the expended (not rescinded) sinews of site. Never subtract the mirage of a fossil from its socket: to gather bundled ground long after the core is to offer the veering of core to an earth of its rounded disappearance. A nest of orbital disappearance forever a non-clearance, but craggy safety-ground fused at the departure module.

Socket in bowl
greeting forgotten
joints. Not a trench
shield but a vertical
trunk yield repacking
the horizontal, cross-

staining the ascent
along ruination

transition fossil from
positional forest:
wrecked or slaked
to accord a clasp

6

Tree portion always before its orbit, rank on rank of socket-seals bereft as earth's unintact integers: broken off as grooved forward, encompassing all the secondary comparisons of removal. Degrain topdust in favour of projective tree-root but magnify the linear scotchings of a ground's absolution: they flare a vanishing onto, the chamber of hollows is harboured at burden not displaced, but takings from place beset to place.

> Difference's non-transfer
> of finite catchment,
> disappearance with
> addictive border, re-
> partition at a
> stony predictive order

Became flushed out-forest tender with the nestling gyrations of impact branching wide a naked site: doesn't close over on flesh-empty but offers a bowl of extraction towards a filled at remove, where horizon convokes a coast's inherence derived of trees. Some remote itinerary redepthed as its semi-tunnelling skewer binds beside surface.

> Gouges a clotting of
> future bore, root
> stalk in rock
> of the empty tree

You also seed root privileges where you will have had a socket re-entering the empty, a rockgroup grasps reportive surround, in its clasp visits abroad with breasted cordon of the pre-empty. Stripped together with primal identity solves a root upon local domain, no non-recipients could ever seem too close. Socket for an operation tempted towards unreachable host, until open mound was the fullest receptive duel in bowl.

To broach that socket
variable I had to
uncommit the host,
surprise defeat
as come to port

Not a slash on its behalf names root, but calcified wrap of a softly depleted trunk: dis-sparred not counter-deflated. Once you've done shirking the kernel put it in the root of its (irreversible chute) stone-cast releases. And exclude any *retained* roots, let them now become the foreign body of horizon.

In pitch of a socket
open to places, don't
outchange root any-
more than a vertical
will rangefind its
intrusions across
 counter-beddings
of source

Yes, site-system with usual start (jerk) at root: creates an empty object (horizon abstaining the open line) containing options for a crater's further-empty, its farther filling than. Post-install tree target (as trajectory of compressed root) and thicken the socket that soon crease-empties the whole aimed absence nar-rowly onto an entirement of horizon.

In a treeless place
all their jointure
nests in hollows
of unerased rock

divestment of ten-
ure arcs its pro-
jective requests,
assesses by a mound
of local devoted
absences

no tree as if
caged, pressed
out along flight-
registers of a
window once nest

Revealed inclusion-bodies if all appear empty upon bright field, a socket was whole in floor to a chairside root. Dry socket, its root figments for clean leaving, relieves a fragment of cleaving direct the access across a cupping of rock. Implements the ghost kernel free-wheeling the rounds of limit until it disappear a second turn (all stony indication) within.

A root's target seat
(settled empty) not
neutrally unoccupied
once launched, root-
less trunk poor lost
returns in the se-
verest hollow of hold

7

At gate ajar in rock draws out through trees how they defix there to snatch the names of root off stance, non-severance locks into the open, the focal scratch of tree surrender. Not drag the code of interest but immediately empty it from bowl of origin, repairing a fabric of the secondary, participates at entirely calcified giving-on.

In order to delete
wood, select upon
an open sediment,
a coil of having
belonging out-
fold the tree

Admittance to a neck of stone is transposite dip of open stance, but in active distance where a shaft was fitted, pitted across the fusals of stone.

Domain drives past
attachment and then
settable: ripped node
can parse rock
for its open handle

Tree debased from easy creation but never anti-dependent: rather, a tied rocket of absence deep pocketed in cupped stone, the flange there is in zero. Of the disappearance a sort of ratchet is worn to folding a tree's step from empty recurrent bowl. A plug outwardly, the delay sent ahead, disrepair towards a tree's daring not just ripped onward but sheered back.

Enfabric the tree
at run-time open,

embowled but not idle
against next forest
cover: from now on
an inverted pan-
oply of stone

Unstocked bowl built from same-source tree, rock-implanted on a secondary surround, in amazement awaiting a here counter-enigmatic: not confirmed towards open void but before some main event drop, the scooped materia of participation.

Socket dresses over
a failed globe's
peeling whole
of distance-connect

Begin a new floor of slot, open a socket at the lapse in tree: the stead is tiled in breccia bedding the collapsural surplus, but pointing out of hubbed piling the way a taper of tree does.

Rifle a chimney
thread by fold
out of abandoned trunk
vacant truth re-
confirms its
cratered platform
is propped, the
saline scum engrains
in incremental
thicket

Descriptor leakage to ensure a socket poses, open source projection (faithful disappearance) is at stillage of crater edge, gantry by surfacing rock.

Hinge the lost
now, open place
of the breaker bar

That cavity's binding address defaults to an empty string does but act on true mapping knots. Green trunk becomes arbitrary pipe were it not for a prompt beaker deflected off yawning socket.

Entire forest shut down
on what these nests
of rock requite at
non-empty rind,
it buffs horizon
with sheen of site

8

A trunk drowned is a focal loss nearing: resultant empty bowl meaning local host. Twisted out of embedding until something here discloses the abutment of socket, no wound not a soft wrench rapping on primal support. The basic premise is for lost kernel not to rebed, but hollow out as lightest upright vanishing along persistence.

> To pool a housing
> round you, un-
> disperses
> abandoning cluster

Trees wiped hard by won texture, guiding a kind of invariance-to-place as brittle stonework, the unstaggering spars of a site's frame-weave. Socket of fallen tree goes forward into place as unpurged blain of stone not any later excavation. Time stamps as open compression its extension vacating on site, but without unsnaring the world wrap.

> Mask ruins root, a
> crater runs as nobody,
> how this naked task
> of hollow face in-
> forms beds of the
> rock in shoot

Candle-socket damped to encradling what is flame-like inseparably in tree until it tongues a greener apex. Stark grappled sources, grip emptied at dense surround, not contentless in grab but with openly faithful disembedding: rind of a disappearance not bulklessly drifted away.

No offering sill
that doesn't step
to the desert
attraction of tree

Impressed by absence, coved into stone by a hollow aperture's tenacious unfillable, the socket recenters a salt-sweep of fallen rind, stone hoop whose vacancy is deep grounded by fled tree.

Sapped tree scalloping
unsteep stone

Weak socket won't hold the tree's ghost steady but clasps its turning away, cratering what counter-dipped along the injection-fade of post-verticals: protection along the way. Self-closed by opening to socket what was bowl of recessive horizon, once trees drew it aside that was burst groundball rounding it.

Opens outrightly
post-empty from
never unset

These abandoned woodland stands don't practise creep, by belonging to absent stakes they stab at attending rock. To say that a fossil grove closes on its preliminary at a favour of departure through site: the boning radials of an horizon imparting.

There were no stumpy
fossils but hollow
bowls of landing
arising into
cellular fit

The extraction wake of a trunk is starker orientation than unravelling the mark, is harder travelling within the combs of bearing up the lightened rigidity of a puddled site. Where trunk vanishes into structural embrasure, it is its shown abandonment which condones the beaching of these verticals, what off-grained any beseeching of cordon: resource trunk diverts upon horizon the outdrop.

Intimate location of
trunk-loss please do
indicate harsh forest
events, a bowl's stress
strives extra havening
throughout shelf

sparsely the enhancing
retrunks a gathering's
chamber of rock:
in open rack of vert-
ical contentment how
site is spent to stone
giving scoop of tree

Lean Earth Off Trees Unaslant

2008

Human being for the Greeks means belonging to being by way of understanding upsurgent beings in their stand.

Michael Eldred

Trees push toward sky, and this sense of pressing upward is vital in forest appreciation. There is, of course, a ready scientific explanation for such loft.

Holmes Rolston III

Tired of not aligning myself towards horizontality—
and with loathing
of the hills' restlessness

Andrea Zanzotto

Hence Deleuze mis-reads the line of flight. It goes just as much upwards with the trees as it burrows along with the roots of the prairie.

John Milbank

1

Binders breaking upward from the closed recess of slope. Tilt-space slides arena but undergoes sweep accorded trees. Abutting the bias proposed forest to new rind: if slope-cover is spine unfettering a rake, the contour heals right through whatever stripes it unaslant.

Slope heaves, the tree-crowns waive undulation from a straitened haven: within all thinning machinery of a world it sustains what covering access chastens slopes. Against full scarp trees mark their own scuff fault.

These slopes were never easy but don't induce on empty mound all reclusive lyings down. A loose bank suffers important vertical cavities where leaf in vortical quarries won't be cramped out of the upright.

Emulate a forest disturbance of naturalized sags of the land-base, here there is no redistribution but a difference of native (vertical) implement.

Trees grown on inclined terrain don't differ from horizon but buffer perpendicular the horizontal secretings of surface rapture. Joy to such common published standings.

High stature outcome was never less than weakness resorting out of slope, timberlines cleave the windstorm cripples, present erect trees at the more protracted sinuation.

Firmly scarce on the vertical, offers relay of edge sheer reverse inference, that shelter is not foresworn in spearing it so spare. How such uprightnesses are unscattered where the groin of slippage had no arrear of selection.

This terrestrial sky isn't pine-forked but sucks onto itself sheer darts of tree. Not a losing return given out on earth, but solely compromised by a mazelessness of vertical poise.

As trees stand on the unrucked side of their falling world, where slope is how a foliar rising carries to spillage (in the heights), not simply its truer plunging of a stunted abyss.

Conversion of bare slope involves its planted comparison, how horizon looms tall derivatives at vertical secondaries.

Thin new uprights or counter-gluts to gradients of famishing the slope out of its untransition: are these poles so transitive?

Skeletal tree formalism but enough verticals abrupting salient cover over slopes not more strongly randomizing their desertification. Verticals were correctives of the offerable not its decisions: limit-indicators so tokenly the free incidence of.

No slope leans up against a tree of its times. Incurvation giving out is singularity newly encumbered, the differential simmer of upgrowth flames a toppled margin unsurrendering porch-height: standing lights across a diagonal shawl.

No slope-deficiency symptoms from such pointing-off. A chute gentled by lightest ascension of root-trait, verticals come to rest (if anything) in a less steep dealable turbulence. Where the unstolen damage of earth is all the sorely upright.

Steepness betook no substrate of angle until a girth of pension-wood lodges long-trunked in staying the projection. Slanting files of wind are reckoned so many vertical squalls of tree.

Bottom-land ravine-stripe, that the prime hazard of embankment was probe of its being stripped of a diremption hitherto habitless. No naked slope is prostrate as such, its strata given out exposed to propelling pine: how a sky's carrying eye is saved a grove's lidless swarm around the unslanting.

2

Trees disclose hillside by a plantation's vertical jet within an apex non-hold repinning it. Shelter is the extenuation of curving grain above a gravity pillar's shorthaul, a hollow already pierced and fuelled empty by the vertical.

Slope likens these fluted narrows to trees, unclonable reed in the resemblant stalk. There is no interscree once clad in the self-reducing share of standing stock that disallows its pitch of shard.

This standing from the horizontal up a brief stop exchanges a plate of substance for a keyed slightness in offering: what can be promised if the offer gives out at an actual tapering of any other possibility.

Oblivious range aslope incites a discontinuity effect in close-grown trees, rapid vertical distraction, steeper (sheetier) anti-arcing.

The lines of separation quoting slope to tree-garb grab that one knot which tapers, leaving out the twisting hub of dearth.

Material in any decoy sloped right across, a major inference is upright puncture, or breath of crown jointure which cues no injury.

So it might be due a cure of unripe retort that trunks don't sway their turbulence, but convoke penetration of slide. But an unhealable coast of slope staggers, the trees are hit stark upright.

Sharp slumps clawless in resplay other than defended tree-roots and so got to feed finials, the grasp of going no deeper than rebiassing the lean. That roots plot tree a position possibility of curing the spot.

A slope's severity its own complete envelopment, in woods cut to margin that reveals the difference in tree measure: this convocation has the one primary root undulation owing erect facia.

As trees will tilt the wedges but find their transforms unportable from the first, earth's secondary (scarce) lift.

The state of tie is the sort of vertical stuff (staff) put through on earthen veer.

Long-leasted woody uprights, slope renudation only at the crests of a taller quailing: tilt of slope is all stems fending from tortical. No glade speaks holt upward but upright slender nub to.

Of itself tree-height files singular steeps against a gully's breaking depth, that the cracks don't heal but in unsolved tallness a smaller earth loses breadth to sky: latterly unrifted at the no leaning, lends sky a screening or vertical rarity gifted out.

Slope isn't much habitat but shelter so occurrable off vertical request, an unenvious pine puts slight pinnacle on the crust: coarse stems manelessly clad in scant (unlent) leading.

In the roll of a plantational billow narrowness is thinning-out from a foliage counter-abstaining. Forest relay doesn't add its soils to any thickness at large apart from what the horizon suffers until too thinly caught. A pace of soil creep leaps the compensation, packed stems releasing it upright.

So firs without stinting flake out these heavy sides onto sky, only the slope of it still naked went stunting over unreliances: now the trees lean direct on the vertical by stubbing it beside them, uprights can be any sparser shaft at all. Tall to tall not a correlation but the parsimonious full encounter at this outer conventional reach. Harmony participates that resistance tapers off the crests of it.

Clamp of slope is bait to tree-flyer screening the abrasion, the vertex-greenery of upcast forest bolt. Trees could only release radically upright the root-penalty of earth, at the least of its proponents this apposition sows beyond the bent of ground. The stem counter pleads upon its needle (formationally under-cut) an original scratch of edge.

Effect of rising minus further gradation, more not less on the perpendicular road, the throw of earth jacked along its cast. Since there were no steps rooting the earth, what gives direct shaft in trees.

3

Trees pale in knot but nowhere in cooped flux of them, not-bending swivels a sky foldlessly relenting. Leaning skyward can't suffer on the slant, only drawn off slope by the unholdable intimacy of vertical separation.

Stunted trees but quickest to retrial the parallels overhead, a grove of points in stack of the direct picked distance.

Terrain knows its cloud-spine is dispossessive launch, how the counter-lurch was navigated once all earth steadies unafloat.

Falling upward the more pressive trees became, firsts of a bed sprung in narrow vertices of a pristine tallness not beaching. Among these stalwarts is earth's visible-shelterable become the visitable waves of vertical exception.

Unaslant marginal trial around the exuberant crass of trees, binding the wind into their heard pitches so as not to quieten it. Soon only sunlight will readily slant its steepness among safely cheapened verticals.

The way earth doesn't spend out in the turbulence but frees up a weak consequent amid standing derivatives: differential uprights slow-presenting slope to a vertical opening.

The frame of surge lightly clads its chided direction: no laterals could cover this irregular ground and still harry the upclasp to such a continence without hesitating however high the edge touches over root.

Trees call from deficient horizontal bracing to risk the rising embrace of. Without entrance, outside founding hindrance.

The leaning jeopardy of a saturated world has to compel itself light by a tallness driven in the sway of, learns thatches of narrow masts mean raring vert, surfacings upface of it.

Trees tail upward, drop a disappearance in at its vertical poor. This grieves earth with not so much a world as the bias of horizon sweeping onto gift, or what sets a meeting upon the shelter-pin of exact projective pelt.

Block geometric streets but row the solitary upright by not steering across: we are of the same poverty as this outgrowth of earth spared for an unbending.

Leanly direct rising, below shelters above once there was merest barrier of presage. A film of sky is reeling within a slope's translucency tubed, roots no longer spin a naked mulch where so much unwrapped coil has gone vertical.

The one spring that won't hurl itself off earth is differential haul scarcely lading a knowing in perpendicular stick. Trees surmounted their own lying against the grain of world, poorly astretch of an unstricken break into taper, at the offerable vanish of upright.

Attend simultaneous intimacy, a buried belonging turned out on the tall stem of its overing frequency. No score of exchange, but reciprocal slendering of the murk's blue-green.

Horizon itself as gaining on curvature, but from a perspective which bolts upright an earth not buckling it on: how a slope doesn't collapse but falls along its own scansion, against which trees tuck integral stress, commonality of differential point.

Cut an arc aslant but there grow immeasurably through it just what runs out of tallness, missing nothing at its unbent. On straight knee a tree's extreme fleeting close, not fleeing the vertex pool in scooped drag. Fabric of call out of the piled wells of remade scope.

4

In straights they pare against declivity, counter-style any dragless curtain of summit. Not the cover a slope is, but how trees convoke where slippage heeds the dawned bristle of horizon.

Theirs can't have been a precise leaning of woods, tallness assigns contusion deriving an earth without robbing its buoyancy of poise, a raftered float of gift out of indifference.

Hoisting one unreleasable lamination above earth in a straight stemming of gift? Slant was groundless once the correction of swerve is far along root-verve direct, uptake of vertical latch: not bent across chance but a hatch opening desire at proprioceptive edge, abides the stab in orientation but uncut. Do trees feel the staff difference, heal the leaping plane of its inference?

Single jointure between what draws earth's defigured surface and the approach to a pinned shore: a world deferring to what is too long away from its own differential.

Vertical stride compressed an earth's way of incline: ditched origin rears a contour-step obtaining a mite of unselect horizon. This lancing tallness is an abridgement of nature, accepts on erect interminability what is each final stem of the offer.

That the naked (scarred) bounce of earth becomes green bar thrown at the newer hiddens. Earth spine from which rooted things fall out, face up along the preventing verticals, no assent is nearer to perpendicular thorn than this anticipation.

A portion's nape sheathing world is the common telescopic participle of standing upright and disinclined together. A tree's point is not to chip the clouds but divest earth of its clipped trailing.

Neck of taut trees not so reckless as to wreak a world on rugged extrapolation: pines crane to an unenmity zone standing out in extra pole against any paradigmatic dipping or sapping.

Disobeys the slope-force of earth in field, a pole towards the uncrooked tip of slightness in the ascendant. As gravity hosts a centre out, its irregular currents above the granular seek of narrow slipway at this hoisting wave. Onto uncoasted sky unlike rising, unlike denial of adjacency.

These come in microbars of a world released from its grids of slope, blinking the betweens of multiple barrier, openly textured by screens got across the lean of slithered hurts.

An entirety slit to coherence risking the verticals of horizon, not a cast light rinsing but its looming slice of the glint.

In undeflection the trees as close to unbarring the declivities of world absorption as they get. Resolving earth's curvature across the steepness-leap they make by not curling any further into it themselves. Is this how terrestrial suction flows otherwise?

Conversion into its proto-crescence: that laps elongation at the feet, to foreshorten by stunning it erect, centering what fails to leach horizontally. Undistributed ease of vertical success incites the fear of it risen in peace.

Where world-hold could be shunted by redundant turbulence of pinned norms: until a spate of upright trees actively sculls the rift towards parallels of its ascension. How any scansion of end lines up vertical steps of filling the stop at up. No nurture can fulfill this far.

Lift stalls in its loftprint and banks knottedly before horizon as the taper gets retracted into sinew bending for reprisal. The ascent not the least exempt from prior instability but same source set upon a hardship of direct scantiness to edge, mast-hood goes seamless at erect the crease of edge.

Conviviality of trees in upright flue greets normative horizon-storm: fire in the root is smoked out of avoidance, free horizontals crackle in the eye of the vertical. A lull at the edging is happier stability once a collective takes it unexpelled to the uptorn.

Admitted into the quandary of the radius of horizon, taut quivers have no other towering jointure of defection.

What won't stand up riots all slope for cover. What grows unbending sows a different spate upon the drift. Which mustn't grow tall without sending out in single shift.

5

Masted insecure but no wavering the approximation. It is the unaslant (a non-sealant) which hugs the givenness of not a root. Vertical counterwave of trees goes frontal with unadmitting margin, but already entered in the unveiled face of. The trees sting heights on the cloth but drape their own shoulders, are prone veils not slanting away from such vertical die-back.

Earth dips or flexes but arises to its own stark alliances of shelter: nor do the generations of trees as such but only at their siting's seedless collective of lift (the pines unsown in their stoodness).

The earth won't have seeded a rift back on itself, nourishment stays in tube at the stakes of its temporary trees: they stole like a nap towards horizon, what accompanies this indirect terrain can be spread, laid on the interim of an indebted surface.

Obtaining in their uprights more than can be intensified: the tensile of trees is in direct stretch given out at a levity of earth-slump freely abraded, cageless in this running out to the unsupplied: in spite of a resourced reluctance, triggers the unaslant.

The earth takes aisled refuge in these vertical compressions, sizes toward expressive glean an unleaning. By ground (not geophilous) generously unhooked until standing immoderately below the arcless upper air, at the stilled tip of the reduction.

Closegrown is unreliquished directory of reach, a crown faring the toss or drape without stripping the verticals out of its stream: any slip over sky is tippage a whole proneness upon the offered danger above.

Earth allows this safe standing to be equated against it. Inoffensiveness can't spurn the burden manifest in trees, how they hum horizon at a co-infinite diminishment of their tapering reef.

Constant substitutes (trees) of an earth nakedly rolling by declension of abyss/peak. Won't consume these absorptions by relegating cover to surface: live out the site of spoil by keeling it toward vertical grain.

How pines surpass the earth's own leaving off by inciting what horizons it at another stricken behalf, and the blow was vertical.

To entall a world is to suspend any reabsorbance of termination, this taper failure receives its needle off the curve, acuity continues to fin. No trees burdened to thinness are fined in the heavens.

Terrain pletion foisted on its sole swerving way. Trees serve themselves a surface of these abysses but scrolled up, crushable not unfolded. Entwinement is tinged at a rootless sky but presses it with a poling quickening enough to see each deletion hoisted.

Once trunks stall at the upright they no longer improvise but tell the speculation: single tapering pillars collectively aburst, filled from earth but unfuelled straight to its leanness elect.

Lance-bitten with root traction, a shoot at horizon's being without, what is exposed can risk the sheltering storm of uprights, untender attracted norm of stems standing.

Pooling horizon by green vestibule, direct pulling shafts of the unbarriered. A tall company leaving the interstice simply enough for bright nocturnals, stars of it brink the slope's contour absorption a spiral stair away from integral incline.

Deliberately assarts all born of induction. Earth's bedded reach to horizon must kneel its yet-to-be-planted on the proof of a vertical ridden.

Create a random arborescence, the root is regarded a self-avoiding sequence of high adjacencies, from plotting such edge the connector is acyclic: for non-root vehicles there is no difference of rest from the zest of holding tall.

The hills in need of vertical offence (in tree), slender debarring not braiding the core but gone equal (partable) shares with sky. Saves from following-along sitting curve any swerver survivor-grid that might abandon whole hinterlands: until the upright stigma of a ground aslope detains it beckonable.

6

In the oblique detriment a shadowless play and fall, until this toll of the tall-identifiable is short but tapered haul. At the periphery of an entire arisal no tree smacks its head but flees on behalf of the reach of sub-soil to tip.

Any counter-rise is less a curb than already posted across the plummet of the way, these slivers do send forepath up the verticals of air-current: how the horizon itself is uncrowded by what forest jostles against the sector-plunge of a reabsorbent earth.

Real sticks were not among the missing, not thrown upward to a farness but pressed highly charged towards: obstructed things (rooted in bypass) at last inexcludably playing out a dearer directional.

A spine of unbelonging throngs these hosts at their vertical giving out, then relearns the gift of spine: how pine's sting is gentler outcome from encumbered origins than groundly battening on a populous sink of parallels. Vertical bines have earth ungrasping as it flaws off the curves of itself.

Leaves at wrist but creep of tree becoming drawn in long vein cut into shares of a jointless ascendant. Knuckles had never been this direct at touching up, root not arising as knees but now along slim terminal terrain.

Slewing of trees angers the slant run-off, delays a landfall's apartness until it points collapse through the vertical of its co-inherence, such straight dues (appointment) from any shiftless non-clearance.

A standard bringing on of edge until unakin to frame, keener field than slope: perpendicular how scantling its scape shaft, overdraws on plumb orientation bolt. Not hedging the steeps unlike the ground's own billowy crèche of cover.

The tree stands at the obstacle of its own orbit, from rent of earth to a deferent piercing of all that falls, cooler ceiling off that grain of retirement, shelter a vertical grist in the seam of flattened tissue.

Trees won't lace the earth where a columnar crayon stencils the outset, lineation through all that subsides marked on the horizon's seizure. First fruit of the patient tree is when it writes up how earth is not a recleft but clothed in sheer cliff of vestige to horizon.

Trees in grief of their straights but exposed in storm-section as a very stanchion-midst unweeping, still rising in guise of final cordial stem. Stretching the gifts I had not owned to bend, directly struck at the tree-crown's pincered globe.

These high tunnels are the rains of foliage onto sky: because the chance of a vertical spray before horizon is no bend of tincture colouring the wind but a greener margin intimately retrieving forward its departures over earth.

Skies would be unable to rest (revest) above a compacted earth trailing off aslant. Sky as such was not to have been stunned behind a screen of trees but is reskinned across their fixed rods propping onto it. What there is peeling abroad from the embedded hood, a thin lustre upwind of it unaslant.

7

On earth ailing in its harness where the trees counter-fall, pull to deft ongiving among dark ungroping files. This barrelling besets the tumbler of blind shadowless surface, its former naked insulation.

The earth holding loneliness without a splinter from its stand, not heaping abed of but keeping aboard the linear tide: climbs what trees don't *grow* now that they stand erect ajar.

At mid-tree indictment there's no column extreme target. Lines correct themselves aslant but wait vertically, the spine ceasing on setting up high to the slight.

If the rooftree isn't strict a whole sledge of earth will forfeit its slant-street: woods rhyme this on their tallest affright. Not bending their topmost youngest but unaslant as though there could be no reprisals over a cradled verticality.

A tree-scraper with the hitches of lean-to off land, how green to advance non-inclined, now pitched at remand of vertical boxing. A share in the stony outreach until there is obstacle of an overhead, such fraughtness in its pilloried (pillar-led) releases.

Stroke upward into forest for sway of central bite: fir trees delve into light for not committing its radial diagonal.

Where the beech ply upward agent against slope they don't tie vestment as vertical coat: it is traction recedes centre, a world's periphery lets itself be pulled the way from. A shoulder of the upright heeds universal tenor at tumblings of earth in bouts of earth.

Silent stems per unit sigh of slope. In straights of sliddenness tree-lift sparks truncation from any wiser framelessness. Not trees out at plume but tapers guiding ground until its giving on.

Only a forest upsistence can vertically pretend the slack: finds the unwinding wrap pulled to where horizon isn't peeling, across unfiltered waves of a clenched ground-away. Not bending over what was remittingly scant tent of earth.

Acutely aslant, drenching the terrain in the unlifteds of advancing drain-off, former trees cross the urban plain by bending but don't intend their bulge for any cavity of coated sky. Done spending more homes on the roofless slopes where trees cannot stand.

My shelter shuns trees up their silent verticals of leaving off, the bunched salient of pleading squat. Deserted plantation aslant a city, the species of power-lean I bleakly favour whatever the earth happens to be spilling.

It is the tip which nods the open, trunks were all wrangle of horizontal clearance. Lateral branches became diversionary by ungreeting (mimicking) a usable exposure in the play of deporting it.

The tree is an abstract tip plotting the outside verve of a shelterable array, each trunk takes to interior concreteness stories of the unaslant.

Every earth a cuticle on extended cover by emptying the coils of tree: brevity lengthways captions unstunted skies, briefest disappointment directed from entire spine.

High pine doesn't slant where the roots are left, connected where they grapple cross-wise but uncontesting a recommitted transforcive source below: agile taunts in softwood as ever free for unrandom climbs in limb.

A mistrust (dragshirt) weans its vert but grows plantational at the vertex, a perpend withstands the droop of unfillable spaces spread across corrosions of source: bred upright upon the decisions of rift.

Easily erodable slope which can lineate woody piers to the hilt, concede forest rim recollects skies outright off a tide unsilting which banks of earth spires are reborn to.

Pass through tiers of barrage pole a slant displacement furrowing up the ridge. My keeping close to the surface the hoist of arboreal creep reguides as narrowest tree, post-grades an earth tumult as grateful for any unburrowing recoil.

To terminate in shelter's vertical is to pinfold the skylets not dilate the correlation (pillars not elating any wider than could be capped within the bay of horizon). Tall timber is fresh flex of standing the connection. But no splitting of region into spatial tree, the index is outright locality unaslant.

Roots Surfacing Horizon

2008

Je t'ai cherchée dans les endroits
Où la verticale
Voudrait s'allonger

EUGÈNE GUILLEVIC

Horizon must no longer be thought of as merely the 'frame' of the originally given, but as something that permeates the originally given content as well as the beyond.

DORION CAIRNS

"Remain true to the earth!" Yes, yes. But our destiny is not to be cave dwellers sinking a hole in the ground, but to find our way to the surface of the earth where, standing upright, we exist above ground between the earth and the sky.

WILLIAM DESMOND

heroic spin beneath subsoil
. . .
a half root elasticized

BARBARA GUEST

Note

The roots here are *tree* roots, however much the above-ground aspect of trees is mostly ignored in these poems. But what would count as 'above ground' when the surface is thickened and inflected by the way roots colonise it laterally? Horizons (the visible horizon, not a soil layer) are hardly detected any differently, but does exactly the same poverty of surface go bare-faced to horizon? Perhaps where this thinness is networked or (be)spoked by roots something of what a surface is before horizon is altered, nurtured rather than simply induced? And the presumed verticality of roots might then be not just a matter of sustaining the trunk above, but have as much to do with the ways roots are typically displaced across a surface which they also reinforce or array: that very pared-down frontal aspect which is what there is to engage with horizon.

1

Infinitely finishing surfaces unrequitable at horizon   facing up another tenure how famished in extent   gives quittance to such brittle unsurrendering, continue long the gauze of a plain   once reft of its spore of root, surfaces sieve their mesh like an infill unconsigned by attainment: embedded horizonwards, signed offerable

imprecise union where resistance engrains a non-eradication as incompletion on behalf of

roots feeding near surface
these pens (no orifice)
open an irregularity
of attachment-to

Roots may expose less themselves than the hollowness of their embedding cooled at a surface's new gambit   how it can no longer play the flat reproducibles of release

if roots knew their own secondary growth, the woody out-crop would undergo tertiary girth, an increase in surface verticality   such roots will stilt the soil arch out of its remissive spread

banking a station towards
attachable groundlessness,
there beckoning enacts
the very nape of recession

Uncoverable root, to bulge in the air's swerve incises the shadow of earth but not naked of attachment   reckons the care of horizon, travail of ravel to the offer of recessionals the face is flaring down amongst thieving roots but offers topsoil a sieve of itself, a texture at which to be simpled by horizon

> where tree-roots break surface
> ground is no sooner rent than
> quoted out of its plane

Not root dormancy when it comes to surface adoption   the season is full quiver wronged by vertical touch   ebullience of hit layer trembles the narrows off horizon's bed but daren't pull anything pyramidal across horizontal infrastructure   a larger flush of debris might need to be petitioned by more than this spanning

roots back-surface without de-exposing horizon   this guised space exits with strange radiance for any insufficiency obedient to its climbing out

> penultimately columnar
> or unreach vertical enough,
> incompletion transmissible
> commonality, ascension in
> a dumped touch of itself

Where roots bend for surface they won't give the superficies a run at accelerate missing content but expend upon the empty catchment one whole zoning shelf of the least of the recurve

swollen vasculars of rigid revision (root) make sub-dermal bulges the promotion of soft-met horizon

> paring away at paradise
> until the sheddings are piled
> roof of root, or sheer un-
> riddance does embed
> a cut to the pitch

Roots given lateral assumptions of an entirement of world-scarcity, dedicatory horizon as whatever can be counter-braced thin enough for surface

less surface to root than shining any apparency (inherency) in the face of its fallen flat on abyss   still to come in the order of fibre or spring a penultimate sill at these levels   by blistering the sparse rungs of surface they plunge a draw (intension) across reserves of disparate (vertical) storage

finite reticulation that something re-enters, universally laid out prior to such lengthy offering across a world surface   foreshortened (released) now at the field node of the nearest vertical

no grounds of soil tumult except by loose root   they out-take surface until it circulates as volume towards horizon   what is humped to a chin abuts: won't pass co-finitely under recession of its wake but is fielded abed awake

any level plain
beseeches span
in the palm of root

2

Roots, lie on us by stirring the viscosity of surface, its increase was only raised this far by not incurring eruption as a lapsed concentrate   a finite extension of floor is what throws back the rupture crease to an unseverance, wide horizontal root of it without parching

perform sky-level surface out of almost nothing below until limbed across by lowered blinds of flatness   broken-bulged surface is all that will cross it, unsacrificed in the lateral test

how a world's depth can be shored round in surface risk   what the resistances no further trust any sealant with, can be trans-opened onto a pre-knit breach combing the pores as if they do spread (plead) for breath before horizon

if surface is re-embraced by depth it isn't swallowed but bitten off as depth frontal limit in recognition of the proffering skin of horizon   the deep tap blunders compact slighting basked by way of root to surface

from enterable earth
to a cosmically unsealed,
root rides grazed faces
to horizon, residingly un-
deride a scarce stint of,
transcendence the blind-
ly fastened beckoner

Innovatory at a core of greatest dependence   below the plain's seed-dust is a depth of differentiated desert embedding its capsized scatter down the greetingest

rootal-axile because plenished figure that co-planes surface   if retention is ante-complete it tapers by every new series what is the one undelayed help to a leanness in greeting   refinities that only the one gift is compatible completeness, a lateral beginning role for roots   flexing the horizon they have stayed additional surface for

a parting made for layout itself where the whole *pre*sidual lie-up is horizon on seam

not crater mash upward
but contortion of retention
pommelling the exhaustion

success within stretched
cell (the one skin surface-
ing) over a pall of root

Roots amend depths by surface over cleft   how participation passages at swells of static   the messages leap to the sill of the outcome as displacement would not

scalds the toil of erosion, ebullition of root-dome skims the very shin to be leggy with surface adherence   a matter of outliving the shaftless drift thickly limbed at its plain caption

not surrogate of surface
but truly under an arena
bedded open, barrier-
origin on clear pan

roots that veneer their
stilt until ground,
proliferate how rend-
itions of horizon (dom-
inance) are weakly
close to optimum

Root planing eliminates surface as pocket to distribute its pivotal lessening of depth   ascent uncontaining enclave as roots knuckle surface to no other withholder the capped anchor is a logic of planes by vertical ply, interruption was conscripted from a downward singleness below

holding out a soil-face rather than refolding it prevents horizontal corrosion: horizons wherever endless surface is interrupted at the convertibility of own surfeit

sore grace attended levels with a hump in the stair scour their unriseable much as a counter-flatness roots didn't buckle out any further than this vertical brow

secured in ordinary, rootal
nearface, cleanest exile
from fibrillant layers
deeming only its lean-
ly advised extension

roots satiric until detain-
ment surfaced, surface
atterric since beam of
horizon prefaces

3

Blindness of root visibly cradling the outsake on surface   exsurgence of difference minus departure, whole pillars of dependence are engrossed by thinnest plate   horizontal distillation invokes rebuttal at horizon

the series 'dwelling' cased down by pared horizon   disaster by tractable origin until refaced at trait of root fixed by exit rank   its own motile bluff off banksome exposure

what is 'unthought' in the flatness-decongestant ribs a stay through covering soil, sublimates inference as relational opacity rootal not neutral, the 'sub' behind this vertex versions a spell elational with surfacing, planar pull to an horizonal abrupt universal cell

call of horizon
no sooner discerned
you do have the chosen
noise on behalf of, its
wanted prior standing

Each root fold is a relict of sky deposited on its coils of flat-hold   the elbow out at mimetic surface, not skin but root-trampled to where the horizon ramifies   an infill clinging to field hollow with horizon, letting the ancient hole usurped by aperture hold again

travel of roots thwarted above their element, re-admitted but on soil-gesticular terms: guard against any over-recognition of the called from its forth   horizon as extra transfer is webbed down but as projective greeting releases the plateau's self-guiding a whole leap out

the fronds of surface (distributive trust) become goads of plenty branching out but only as nodal as horizon was   condensity of the flat sheen surface population, what ripples is the transfer from every other density

lead a wad of surfaces
true from such depeelings
(rising) off a
nail of root

Stringy root, hard skimps scooping above surface   but besets a grate before horizon to accompany sandy pleats out of linear revel   roots unsealing themselves cap depth at its cuticle nipple, how it billows contrary to horizontal gatelessness

what was wholly above surface is always less than anything surpassing it, roots offer the incidence of their slightness over   all or crane across surfaces on an elbow missing horizon but fetching its boom

jam edges with what enters
seekingly, haft of gravid
register but now unchokes
a splayed rope of surface
past its pasture, paradisal
scope the rehem of edge

Horizon dis-ascended no sooner crossed with   a motile root's perjective stone, pebble polished on surface for not throwing an undressing over the heights   return flanks at a radiant spit rolling against the horizon curve

humped arcs of distribution the catchwing/hatchbay of an horizon not withdrawn   receding along a co-sprawl of seconded proto-agulation these submerged spindles spend a hulk of patient fabric, a reservoir lifting the back off depth is elect explainer at surface

near to buttress
our own limitlessness
until the expansion
leaves a shelf ingressed

The figment rootal spiral as convex as stooping to surface knows a lug at horizon dedicates across the lob coming off the plains a listening fragment upon its surdant originals

sprung plain was not a stretchable element, is inclement reachlessness ahead of the tack of any lesser hold, without the roots' own stabling quickness off surface joint

roots radial across surface laid it on particles for the vacancies the stub of a tree with all diving tallness beneath, deep-water can't prevent landing universals in such a shallow recoil, the meshable skin it stands in

gift in contingents
from origin, root
thriving for recension
within the screes, surface
has taxings of mound
under the very tree
of arbitrary horizon

Enfibering the plain was proto-vertical in its poverty of commending surface: root convulsions at rest beneath the same dome disparagements of actual tree, its taller fallen short

now that revulsions blow surface over surface for longer, the very skin is more rideable patted by sittings of root shaping with salve the sores of an economy pure surface repetition can never live

as jolts out of retention
seek real stations, de-
traction in depth beached
till horizon forwards it

single scar of rootface
from bare thickness datum
a wafer of infra-delivery
stings upon ground

4

Roots stout in bulbous lamina, not beyond any gap in surface but its
depth pardon   where they feed leats filled from surface as the code of
horizon's co-sequence of over-near difference

watch over me at pitch of the farthest superficial   where it is plucked
for its earth content there is high rootal ruck combing from cover, texture
of horizon according to seam, the exposed cementum

not that root is planing surface but severely quickens a layer rich to the
end of layers   if surface does harm to the depth series it agrees a
discarded flex to whatever grades up against empty sift   as planar
spiralling relies a term to horizon, nothing spends across its coil of floor
but the one twist vertically accosted

in graces attached above
surface, shallow ruin
to where the attainment is

find surface made with
minimal gleanings bidding
below, excision punctual to
horizon's allegiance
of remaining withdrawal

Amputation of root devoted to the motivated glidings of surface even
toward the unrehearsed tread of horizon   reserves only partly uncoiled,
poor shore enough to serve the bulk of gift   slow spining across surface
is surface pricked thinner than itself but risked in the veinings (obtainings)
which distend (inhabit) crevices told of horizon

exposed for what harvest at the poverty of horizon?   assertive scarcity
of the rooting platform that surface regrains its run-off so fibrously
underneath the way, no longer serves the whine of laminar skidding

roots reaped in the inform
of uncut earth, like bones
goading a way from under
the stickage of flesh

thresh their protection
zones way outside trees,
detection of drawn fibre
zooms an endless stead-
face abounding horizon

Roots taller than cascades poor in the soil above them   these whorls of subspoil pan out the exact rim of depth changes   its pitch tender enough to surprise surface with an unenvelopment in its midst   auroral flatness with such roundel embracing features

a platitude that surface performs its mosaic from practised root   horizon must go along with what surfaces ascribe the commonest encumbrance: whether to be rooted lengthways proves extraordinary recumbency, this is what recoils *to* horizon, no longer brittle enough to strike the unmargined

out of proportions roots put to correct stressing of the tree above, root-whorl has its own surfaces to apply   further stacking of its rindquarters heritable against a token ramp of cosmic veneer

prongs of unreft soil upon this stolen planet   perfect levels of a slack difference always crouch enough variables to be passing *under* horizon, pure precession   but let recess call out its vertically unamending congruence

root stretch has forgotten
own tree of it, un-
gently worms out from
under the sample vertical,
gently wimpling in field
another sign-wrap
of the vertical

Surface can't be covered by itself and features nothing other than screen exceptions of relief   horizon into this at pure transition, the dearest convexity a surface has for the disparate doom of itself

root might do anything with floor though only a flap at surface, while horizon sips them both: there we implore some common cladding off the slippage

averted flotation (at root) must be numinous, its poverty of lining an exposure no longer ominous   the surface dipole the sweeter for being only weakly omnivorous   what is within it or over it not deducible from a hunger of skin, for all the spare root of itself crammed to tissue

subterranean cascade
soaks its landing-out
in one shareable band
of whole-world put to
skin's scour, land-
foil surfactant

A no longer rearable planet would outstance us with bulk star of surface: the granules beneath pounded to haze if the roots when lifting towards stellar rarity didn't pole on edge a whole diminishment of depth

as such roots don't picket in slot: a surface brittleness leans over the compression of laterals so small to be snare to   the regard stops where horizon strips everything onto surface, tedding roots until they roll the shaven areas before it

the rap between rootal
confluence and finite edge
knocking the glare off surface
where nothing not arrivable
had ever conducted
emergence itself

5

Ribbed abreast of the throng, broads of surfacing above drift: bony ripples know to the very baulk the currency of their arising   root shirks nothing taken to surface but murks it with the open door of an unreflectant horizon

a bowl of soil laid to empty table on the flat   root as its provisional deputy does forage all the way out but with no schema in the least exit-like

though it pans to within a face of horizon it is not segregated at the before, being without that terminus   but *is* aggregated by a surface-seeker at the terminals of root

not ribs in spate but a
hull to the smooth
peeling, dead central
by all that could crank
thinness about it

Depth and surface do budge to co-persist, both rumpling before the sheer ajar   the sole transversity not pitting against this as newest hostility on the thin is horizon's   root behest leads a triteness of cladding, to line surface on its bad filter lading off horizon

a distributed sheathing along waves of surface transect   once past its tap, root capillaries articulate like an apron reflex, the piercing no longer crying vertical but a surface's eye of horizon

any skin already internal to the face of sky is surfacing sky from off the vascular vantage of root horizons

under gravid soil
an anchor astretch
is chainless to
resurgence

roots crammed the pre-
amble, a loosening
assignment encroaches
surface's final tilt

a soil's high
listlessness no long-
er loops some same
sump deploring it

Restored surface at a cohesive provocation   root behaviours call for waiving the skew, a surface in whole separation if it were not for the projective tangent bundle

shallow nose to core roots appear to but better won at their counter-poise: the pose is inflorescence of floor, seepage onto any untempted grain of   the heady remains of losing against horizon

bedded through a spoilt horizontal whose collusive root came out of horizon: in calluses uncramp the cloy of root in sedimental stances   of the surfaces themselves so husk can settle above the customary broadcast of root

root demean snare
clear a cosmic ratchet
through to amplitude
that inheres its own
external cramping

Cusps of pursing root made sharp niche on the surface's unnesting gait: though pace was horizon's where the rasp of reception is coded between every rib of the signal

understem woven offside feels its own adsorption   flickering plugs display how there is a culling of deeps to place in the breast above

root trudging the grain of site without estranging the glean but set onto fields of reaped surface   all that furthers a vertical clearance out of small caught space

elastic facia all things
once stabbed at last
embays in ledges
a spurt of prehension

nidiculous membrane
fugal of its depth array
the cup of wealth to surface
basely prone fugitive

6

A ribcage of root scaling its pan sprained in crest, requiring a whole surface poverty without the slightest leap over it   these shells are bobbing in surplus depth anxious for extenuated face

swimming a surface with few diagnostic features vetted so far as its zest for rim   but nowhere nearer than a cartilage of root offering the limpid join of secondary repletion   horizon the apparent ineliminable outer tendon

taproot seething to be recaulked at surface might no longer thirst but embroider (bewilder) the otherwise unfetchable reach of things unpitchable breadth of the thread it brings

a first step water-walking
on this great face
was already
three paces of root

not rocking a surface open
but transversely
deserving it, the
lump in the skin
appearing across it

Clusters of defeats cross the supple screen of space   is that display put there by dusts on surface without any sheen of outlet?

roots so close to bearing down on their driving thirst to feed in the dust attenuate a hive of micro-sockets   encase the limbs which an emptiness in ripple will wrap about the fore-niche (once given edge), finding all particles exchangeable but no longer moveable dust of surface among staples not ousting but elongating the repairs, for nearest neighbour probe to the regimen dispersed by horizon   no poorer in world pairing its evens than to be drily capped

exposed to resurviving
the plain, elevate a de-
siccated flap at a pull
of thickness direct

origin-zone bought rapid
taper, surface-of-all
reckoned on its outbay

Loose range of a floor deferring to its breaches of   root this dust is counter-bathed in what will cement a receptacle though scathed to dry out poor   or kept moister by horizon's own unwounding increase

materials existing pin up the beneath just short of receding in height back to flatness over all   belly of attachment on unlevel grounds of letting go, swathe of distance unsigned except as inexistence letting come

hamperings of earth are innovatory because there is oppressionable floor above core kept scratchable by horizon   ditch into the less not reachable but as in availing immense shallows with burden

the opening biddance of root outspanning surface, risking its grudge as only a vertical error should if a world thesis conceives of an equally essential leaning from surface, the bias is rootal

where root is the out-
step, surfaces canti-
levering off horizon
are no mishap

root is whatever
peels its shale
long enough for
the allowance between

7

Netting the crux of surface without coagulating *on* it   speckle with fillet the dirts of array   sending protracted film of texture onward to the thinness of horizon it is about to undershoot

banking on some tumulus of root as a hinge replay about a zero opening in space   it was lumped to portent from summating plugs with circumstance, thickened to be at a slightness intimately level with the vertical in transactional swipe

surface failure to resort to pristine naturalism copiously impends beneath: fine hairs between the stony rate of exposure   sensing a deposition might justly imprint the over-determination of distances, confiding outline on a plateau of enwrapping

here matted by intricate memory of nothing unplaited but what is offered the asymmetry of emergence

counter-sunk or to be
adjoining horizon pinned
to surface by more than
it suffices, enspine-
ment in core health
of a prickly desertion

interminous skin combed
to end of thread
by care of root

A surface tasked by fretful inset (common local root) can't last its global obstinacy out   is barred at a greater accuracy of inclusion by horizon arising off flatness' own roundel obsession subinsula of root-shoe bred against folds a world is rinding   to be read against great bleaches of horizon treading in the focal dirt, dead past surface as gone *to* surface on surf of laminated root   islanded at their limit-infinity on what becomes vertical no sooner repaired to ending-at for given-out

braced surface righted through
endfulness before the
offering recession of
telling a beckoning

Surface is a hide to set before a moving constellation of root   a crablike spurring of soil is scoring the sky for an own faintness by which to be its under-skin   wink back the puckered hoods of upheaval-retrieval

ramification thin-farming to the verge of its profile   remodelling the disclosures a whole thickness sky away, this is the constant of the skin-distance that recepted it

no mere conversion of depth onto density, any thickening is toward replete foundation at a slighted obtaining   what can be unextended enough to set a face to horizon

subcutaneous in fibre lances
surface for its immensity,
reseals it along the fore-
floor: let this counter-
launch go finitely woundless

Crouch to the vertical aligns a content for rootal tubes paling up to the horizontal   a test to be emptied now, not of the void, of satisfied slenders alighting on enough slicks for support   offering that substantiated poverty again at horizon briefly a pr*e*tuberance of binding knot (varnished on surface) brought to a vanish before horizon the contour of spot curvature gleams from knack of root, if it flows over soil it is still within its savour of reprieve swerve in the entire released wedge of horizon will be the same heavy dot of original intruding

unflown stone ramps
root-chipped to surface,
if a poke-hole elbows any
stoop-rod it rarely derides
hunk from brink

8

Brighter amputation of root devoted to how glidings of surface motivate and only then a connascent address of horizon these unreserved beds at full stress are earth masking their scale to, the guise lifted

bed beflakes itself horizon, rootal tendons forsaking one burdened mesh for the poorer (but pitched) cache of soil about its opposite distance a blemish of coating is all the taken ground it has

root-burn is surface
crazing the rim of all
that is unresignable

shallow roots wristy
at counter-sloping, but
not wresting surface
from any flair
of kicked-in horizon

Defends from a planetary suture, the join bereft of roots but knitted together by the row of what ceases at surface this teeming out flat will trail off any brittle absence-from failure of filaments is sharp presencing towards

such frank fabric of swollen surface needn't desert its mirth of horizon as bold welt the cover-sheet feels prolonged a strong weal by linear ribbing: no inflammation lash but that of horizon rubbing

interfacial tension, wherever roots have acquired horizontal skin they grow to a granular vertical rebedding it, succinct as given at surface for not deheading it

a graft of tenure between
grounds and their suing
for horizon, choosing the
heavier lessening
of themselves

at the shutter of surface
an open foot of root

Soils vary to the degree in which horizons are repressed   roots hurry to relief in surfaces by which it is expressed   if a soil-edge finds own feet it is trodden from below, root prints a security for flown roam

impinge the contingency abetted in root, any tangent is entirely surfacing but not the shallow sum of things alone   a harvest surplus must belabour its keeping by root, best satiety of an uncroppable seating at horizon   blind granges don't go limp on surface but are risking the full remainder across

a map of roots visible
on the face of a pittance
at credence, wends to sur-
face admittance: root-globe
will relieve flat earth
of its cosmic seizure

Great surface plane with no trade of its vertical travail   unbroken porterage to multiple finitude as though it were itself severed from the roots which leave it out unburied   one of spinning severals under a rawly located sun

depth hair (shy to shield) of wavy reliance but groping at the crust itself rather than sledging to a crescent rust on a capsule of surface

don't lie across fellow currents on the panel of feature but ply to world these wavelets over its head   a gust of ballast raises surfaces from

beneath the apprised wrinkling of horizon   however deferred, at such
baiting of earth the rim-research of cosmic attention is pre-referred

no leaden root is as un-
cushioned as this hush
on surface, the hard
binding to horizon

in the ample of horizon's
own-world abrasion

9

If surface were broken open it wouldn't be found to be toothed to root but bluntly joinered in plane setting   integral scars of staring onto foundation stay fresher than do intricate joints of avoidance

not cellular with floating root, these vaults were slaking uppermost just before surface is weighted to begin   as though horizon abreacts onto the skin of what summons

verticals can only sprint
at surface pause, be seated
along the rootal hug of
outer-skin curvature

where horizon hunts the
keen-skinned there is less
clotting at the roots

Budding shornward with all that is weathering the ins and outs of surface gain   a fountain of the abyssal given out radially as in root, so no layer allies disrootedly over another   each is actively detailed off the drawn hairs of a thorough vertical wandering

disrepair of horizon will be divined out of us, our holdings nothing without surfacing in bold need from a semi-rigid hob of roots   if surface-pactive then pro-intrudant

a plain stepping on
rubble assumes root
onto the table of horizon:
where else is there a
frailty model for
surface contention?

Rootally florid undertow allaying the brush of face across face: surfaces drain themselves off within a flange of horizon tarnishing the self-made gleam of desertification

these horizons congest more than themselves even while being never wholly spent on us   surface exhaustion is the extra space they keep alive

it allows us to press for infestation even when there is no rift in the uncloaked surface   not sheltered by tree display but solely in a welter of rootal inference

root apart is renewed
blockade which quickens
surface, earth it in
friction so meekly horizoned

Was root emergence any counter-stratification of surface?   roots don't project, they intrude where they're immersed from   a facia has no other parallels to lie over once it has become skin for vertical differences: whether seeing last is not diverted blindly first but sooner beguiles a neo-accompaniment across the asymmetry's meta-visits, the emergency co-releases

root burns itself out
within blank pleat:
surface erected scorch
until horizon felled
it to ash cooled
by the marks below

theft from root
torn towards layer:
the respond is scarcest
cover overlying
nothing like itself

10

Cosmic retention from finitude underwhelming on behalf of   uncon-ditional gift relaid on surface throughout the time series   thin relic of the hand-over present at its constant or empty end but hypernaturally active about the rind

keeping origin starved to the sacral is a way of concurring with relationals deploying a world zero overdrawn   purge of rootal fretwork to the lip of the same seam, its mean edge in means of

semblable faith likeliest switching from root to stem   surface was already counter-attached but the enrichment discerns so little of the award while still below zone   but is given for an arousal of root fully alongside this circuit-breaker of an arrival, scoping it the rake of a before-horizon

a test-bed alike series sacrality, a world doubled up on its own attenuation from root surfacing the fold   emergently deferent repenting the outlay at its deep fore-sheltered offer

compliance of a failure
on its exact position
of cost was nothing so
horizontal, really
a recloseting of a
hosted isolation

we only learn that
by coming at horizon's
root-enshallowed
company of surface

What enwraps bodily is not so much threads of attachment (converted to the ache of final skin) as a future wealth of common mediation already feature-inflective at horizon   shields surface from the continuous cycle of repackaging it, what would otherwise be rimless in the way its ungiven self would have no boding either

not autonomous as without ground but upon the surface ground of its lessness dependence is entire recess unsquandering horizon radiant since co-encumbered

staying close on the earth, not simply to it, is offering squat gift prior to the step of dependence, as much an unshod co-creation as its rootal sign-face

how these surfaces push
their origin to torque
but as twist of emergence
no longer their own trust

a flickering at horizon
is deemed to obsess
finer lashes of
unpeeping root

Thriftwood at an unbared below-surface but steered to emergence by deep handling, no vengeance horizonward   as roots revive scab against any declaim off surface, so leanness of the capping is recrawled globally

shallows prepare for motive or opaqueness at the open end, there to perform a perforate offering finitude   root flexure sizes a chosen obsolescence, scudding onto rift whose flattened infills relay the trench   no sky will undercut while a dome of surface is more universal for its studded mat of roots deep-staved among undipping root the crave is horizon's

infinitely unclothed but
locally curved to the
offering drape of horizon

11

A non-entirety of earth before sky, retrenchment to the fibres of surface not just attired (worn through) but steeped in the cavity coat of root flinging the open from the open   as though roots needed to come up for air but won't inbreathe such gauntness before its horizontal asking

making a scarce tangent of surface's overlay of its own depthlessness already spread by root and trusted to the turn of horizon   a ligature de-immersed in soil will lubricate that hyphen desertible at surface, then reload its rifeness toward horizon

the earth we baulk on, bareness of uninterruptible surface not yet embarrassed (embarrened) by roots, nurturable toward horizon by the supported unreach steepening in hulk

surface seeing on surfaces
might well not open up
what rifts it for scope:
any compound gap will have
de-horizontalised its own

though root domes forth
soil can't behood it to
equal comers but must go
poor to bed

Doesn't shaft above surface but engrafts a shallow maintenance until there is hollowness atoning   horizon infilling all the onward dispersion of a shelfless self

broken springs of root, you never had to be dug out ahead of your sealed spindles of difference   a surface's unquoted middle does get to divide its own in/finity at this sparing slash within the unentered that overdetermination of 'to be' stringy with horizon however slack along lines of the slighting kind, actual generic

> the tree itself above ground
> like freshly rankled skin
> hafting over a dis-
> embittered rootcage
>
> less dark cloth of an under-
> scape than haggle a blot
> fled to surface solely to be
> on terms a planar remove
> grows over it

Roots laid vertically on the pivot of a manifold, the flaw is horizon direct a grounding doorless but not by retainder in the geo-outlook, there *are* windows of racination   though the alighting skims skin before target, the curdled border is transfer-complete

root at its ration of surface   the affront is dearth but actual frontier is horizon venturing cusp to be so frailly out of deep   neap of an emergent

> outclosure of the consummation
> left inexhaustible in a
> finite blockade cost, but
> offered (exhausted) to a dedi-
> cation's scarcer infinite
>
> depth that a surface buckles
> upward without towering
> thick owing of an horizon
> winnowed by root

A root's above-ground is not stem-like   out of its element but still not rhizomic, its remaining subject to a within is what gives ground before surface professes ruched floor at the restrewing be vertical by allowing it a propellant at its plenary corrugation

it is the horizonless which remains contractile, a curtal of fragment on the flat the cheapest roots aren't intemperate, they tolerate (toil at) the ideality of participative surface

the sowns began to blow in upon the desert much was grist but surfaces get to be given out in short-form of horizon

the multiflex of root
abrades linear baldness,
surfacing no longer
adds a smooth-count
to finite affinity

roots aggrieve no better
burden than horizontal
retribution: at last
for a surface to stand
the heights of the outer

12

The mutation-plight of roots ahead of surface but within minimal profile above   not unprobal however slight the citation against totals spread level: among roots the bedlessness is driven from neutral

horizonal forbearance so that surface is less grateful of its soil than brimming from root, less the little of it wholly to be there than a referred slightness of relief   the lank quality of layer put finite-linear to layer quests an infinite revision of haltings piled up frontally, the host gravitrope

surface is whichever depth is uncoverable where emergence itself enlaces (co-dares) the abyss   where surface root-planes attachment on the trestle of exposure, along fluxes which it is for root at the face to defuse

local enmity changes width
between roots, a fraction of
connectivity falters density
awarding the strewn axials
to a root propinquity

root-tool debenture
that pleads no
abstention in surfaces

Reach is prior to any emergence but the tension to engage can only do so upon surface, given the *parked* heterogeneity of source depletion around root   the link to horizon is notch before output or patchy gift riven with a burden of aperture, but perfectly formational of surface at its due work: aslant a reserve of drawing onto world

horizon not bypassing soil pore pathways but profiling them by way of unplantable indigent root   a propping sound of swollen braces knocked onto the tracks, a dimensionality within need of swerve a depth given out in slips

whole root systems
may let go preferentially
on *loosened* desert

soils tarry in the scree
to which horizons
are compressed

Long bethinned to the vertical all told   net soil impudent for root reticulation but wise to surface elation only   humic stutter that such an affrontedly accorded moraine should give facial enrichment   any horizon that waits on surface encroachment is itself depositional

bleach horizon and attract it to world accretion by the co-vergent nodule of basal drift   the unhiding disapparel of rooting it through to any trifle that outstakes the coating

it is an object for roots to obtrude some sunken standing by stay of surface, shielding surface from any gelling over that would want to prise off the next reject overhang

fibered smooth pact, half-
point attachment never a
markable native until horizon

the separative property may see
as much reparation
as disparity

Planar injection, a braid ambient about surface conjugates the thin film whose glistening is flights to horizon no longer resubmersible

a world surface is harsh but unforbidden   earth resites its facings for whatever abatement a root can entreat, all that becomes scarcely nether from prominent abiding everything missed if not threshed onto mediate floor is more storm-prone or clearance-vexed than the swell of it towards horizon having seen to the root trails   immediately removes surface from the buffer zone it should not remain

storms elongate the raising
wound, a pad support
grants suppuration
but retorts horizon

preach surface to a flail's
rehooking, the shaven head
is horizonal grief

Human as strange as rooted, always severely rotated by what located surface: radical gleaning along crush inquests into the current arrest of horizon, fluctuant zest towards adjacency

participatory pittance under the surfaces of its clearance but ribbed and limbed for as much as an emitted layer won't be directly reverticalised: this counter-sinking at a terminally rinsed-out root thinks horizon

commonly the nearest brought to film on which our salvation is allayed in fibrous slice so much thicker than horizon is   intimately pressed enough for there to be no other intent on lessening

root/horizon will uncover
one another their sponsor-
ing surfaces the offering
spousal of violated skin

yet to rid its sufferance
root reseals on surface
binds out for releasing
it stood, vertical brushes
about a pure lateral

roots can't enlace floor
without trusting they do
to a sign of horizon, given
only on surfaces themselves

Between Branches

2009

Aujourd'hui la distance entre les mailles
Existe plus que les mailles

Yves Bonnefoy

If I see Paradise it is between branches

C. H. Sisson

. . . nothing and yet promise of agapeic mindfulness
of all that is; a creative between—between nothing
and God

William Desmond

1

Abreast of the fore, any universe crossing it reaps much lattice by leaving so little of itself out   compound in diminishment, the ground is forward preference assenting intrudant betweens

assess the origin characteristics of branch stepping widely the gaps to a threshold of us   to set up a repository per counter-force of branching is still no more variously invasive than what had opened between

traffic off main staghead not fervent between embroideries   the very outspan is circulating a more finessed brow of the between   simpler full allaying otherwise than the mutual hem of its differences

> the search branches on
> traversity, a re-
> diverse inference of world
> too combed now for its
> former unfilterable difference
>
> earth in flank faith,
> branch it through
> filaments that glean it?

Mutual branch does cede proportion, the constants between are remnant onplay beyond the set but none simulating loose bands   a full ratio of gap fronts participation in splitting harmlessly from distance until it wants a cross-emit deepvein in frangibles of recovery

lengthy clamour of those dawning slights sounds so branch-minimal still redeeming what isn't wholly conjugate once willowed on the through to restrain among the parts that care

how bare this hectic
branching of a tree
gets to be once
its intention goes
admissible between

what pale summit
for an angle between
branches, does the limit
itself blanch across?

Quiet blame between branches we can at least assess that ontological storm, any recess there not in means to be barely adverse   not so much distributing origin as sharing the poverty of fined reach, differential gift still only one narrow beam sampling thin at betweens

how do I block seraphics from being merged in branch?   but notice the revocation is well past the lack of it like any trans-shape not recalling how branching-apart was itself furthering between   nearly as close as this pared density making for a reapparency

packed branches mere code
to the deferable
newness of a world's

a minor plant order
can only reach out
at the lessening fraughts
between branches

No inflection between mergence and original, but common outshed across a scarcity much plied in   is the parsimony method a foreground weakness of clasp or a backdrop stinting withdrawal?   thinning creates little reparation between branches, the transfer beyond distancing cranes its stills across evading dendritic weave is work of a micro-gauze, no actual twist of texture but how porousness gets between any other membraning trust in its own deed of fibre

> heterocladding branches
> sides share difference,
> common scarce source
> at an unscoured between
>
> convex pseudoveins
> ensystem collateral
> trans-constrictions

From interbranch how disproportional to eye of between, this specialism having no other serve than leaving a world in   irreducible to getting bagged to twig or any pastime ambivalence at the lancet knits

however it brooks fiery angles smudged into, the braces won't have become wedged: two branches of the dispersal elation may have become linearly recoupled across the sun but the intimacy between is broadest ingle for intermission

> inaction between branch
> for a multiplicity of
> repose segments
>
> roaming the branch off
> screen complies at gaps
> in homing the rift

Between branches via riches unscored off vernal background coming in for its mark, what the branches won't mount on their textless veins   bands of issuance in a timely clamour unpressed to any mean of latency, the fanlight half-mooning it intends the entire round tincture of globally in between where a world is some repressed entirement only resurgent branches cross the dilation but scold it pleating their caring, dispense amidst field-quirk of uncorrected shelter   no offence in hollow carried between creases a sheer of the whole means

such world smallness clears signal level inference between branches, cross-correlation is reception swayingly out of case   however unamending in filature there is no swell to the wholly outside save at budding a beyond from the between

of its code to be purged between branch, so that place to hand is nowhere free like this unless its mesh of brushes is left ascriptive of the keeping, strips behind gaps

deep intervals seek trees
dense into their thinness
of reach, conflict missing
its fit along wide
caches of branch

A comedy of sky probing its collectives between   a poverty of that sureness letting its casuals be certain hollow lobes unribbed among   radial opens billowy across fretwork of inferential separates, so much in being the cheapest posting to a between

around a tongue of between, the lee of trees   where pledges to a term of edge stay dry, won't snap open   branches unable to keep this threshold widely slighted (dilating the unmet) quite as unsheltered as they themselves

resting between branch
refloats a guise to being
across, in all other re-
moved ways dis-federate

ex-ranges of distant
filter put to intimate
aid of frontal

A mis-density lapping an untied mesh   such thinnings judging be-
tweens inaugurate the bulk role of traverse cross-grown   would you
rarify the supplication between branches anyway sheer?

transition between trees more cryptic than all the other reticent frames
departing branches   any riddle as openly perfusive as this must raise its
firstlings to a quasi-entablature not to forsake the between

dealing in severe but unprone locations once their semi-removal through
chinks isn't absence but slender ramification of betweens they have
already heavily entered

sustainable adhesives only despitely in the way of, branching full domain
to an aside, occasion obstructs over too pliant rejectives between   is less
in the interval dividing expansion out of itself than the diversion effort of
what must traverse/ indemnify each other's effect of self-hollowing

vegetal lancets forfending precrossings of light, at a spate of shadowless
pro-ruption   the obstacles a speckle of the lit at a time, branch delible
once the rubbings of glint have spent between

dissemination of spread-
lings non-rampant
but baiting their
entry-point

divaricates for credo
between branch, its hail
a real extant advocate

Where what is not tenured (filigree) in stiffening a sequence of itself
(never ahead of what couldn't be held out to) offers any texture taking a
part laces of particles on pause spliced until they interpose   penitent
before such foregivings creasing up the expected temporal report

bunching what is keenly uncovered a fretscape out of micro-recupera-
tives   all the dis-cooperations between a sky at vast ascension and earth
going the least of its vertical delta away from a crust of desert purposes

across a grid as not to branch slightly any the less but increase outwardly towards scarcity fuller overlap   non-contraction what wouldn't have held to what doesn't fall into lack, these ramifics were puny spectacle before disenchanted lip, no ordinary swivel of the cross-fruition of enough: in the lesser between a more than whole in slice to be reoffered

its species cut to
bespread, sequence al-
ready pruned by
unwrenching the divergence

poised not on dominant
spring but head in wing
down the branchial, a
perchless between

Shutters all that spaces free-file, taken in the between which do not shuttle, no local focus reduces to meek middling stress clipped to stripe but an open linear overtakes its weave, the recursive gets to refrain more steeply into plight straight through betweens of broadening terminals

idyllic enlacement scouts the very brush of sweeping it abyss, what still lurks to miss its step through the gauze, lesser passage engulfing identical twig tally at a ramified real tender vacuum   forks among dis-solids granted whole pendings of the retention

within the cellules much overlip from chamber but which filter up the scale (in reverse green wilt) a lending of understood scarcity towards   between branches until fed leaks of its failed stanches

branch to arch low
attenuation pathway,
hollow breaches in-
festing local confluence

let the branches of a
tree do rear-guardedly
its redundant organs

Damaged upright skies with inviolate plant arts, this particular unparched risk cures to a between: the branch-instant is not in itself ramified

a surplus immediary derives betweening by getting at local openness   before a crucial unriven is given stress of gap among what is always less than its breadth of siteless release

you go between branch in disparate envelope never in fact fingered by trees: particles won't envisage crossing until partitions become nothing hollower than all sides enface the bifurcation rather than feature into rift

performing diagonals on branch in release whose crossings go to it only on the slant   these hollows are its horizontals in field degree of nil resistance, dis-hasards tuned to glitches (pitch at fault) between

a slender frontage init-
iation by branching be-
fore the main crick of
an unsurfaced between

Intensive branching focal for gap held out, the allowance is passenger on longest-term alliance minus absorption back to net   but what an entire cosmology can grain from its filter   the branches go far out of pitch as real-space over-whole chasers so long as the escapement cribs it between

they form an inlet latch of horizon   slimming its sinking sun to this eye-upon   with no flicking past generic gap that might be induced to gaze ahead of the between

chinks of a reticulate universal likely to become granular in its gratitude for the co-fear of a startle-point   even more can we be surprised without remainder, without raining on the between a threnody of encapsulation

no clean passaging
either except a spray
padding out times swollen-
headed at the between

eviction's fettle got between
branches, not stall-
ing but entailing

Nothing in loop but on brink of awaiting a lace   beyond mediation what is flexing (and flawing) the sinews of divided admittance   differentiate by elective gaps that obstruction might be in no way of of   without collapsing back onto solid-branch material remittance   glade in minute stay of dressing a gauze to it

reserve charge rather than thanked resistance but switched on-branch, intermedially the hollowing bows across the bridge of its stretch

to intersect by infinite reversion locally followed   in one impoverished loosening even more concrete a loss is offered to material selection, where the release should only overtake on its limits across a vertical

whatever between branch is evasive won't be materialized by any revised affinity: the distribution itself was hyperbolic in keeping to one side of suspended origin whose braiding has now given open pleat to place

back-split branches prove
unarrayed thud is live wood
getting across encelled
into its failure, eyelet
at the heart starlight gauze

animation between acrosses
resorts to no self-suspension
privileging each lacking

If depreciation in green were to multiply off its blades, but those indentations assign a lane of reserve   each time stuttering by lure, these are the consents of spaces of repair   between branches equally sighs the tree

affrontal branching seeks a co-debtor in snatching from gap   needs a whole tree make-ready for its differential leaching really tiny nothings in loop but through to its needle-assent in unhemming the outline of all these betweens up the very lee of branch-pierced foliage

not reaching or congealing its central embedded relatives   the relata obtaining edge of field were for whittling a greater light through no alternative trees

attentative imploration defers but assaults, to the crossing brushed no substitute other than this subsistence on-behalf   not in half-shares but entirely across its reference (sufferance of tapering field) through an edge of world at chafe-centre of the between

swerve right off
syncline, pledge implex
repletion, so betweens
themselves don't
rest in cordage

already a suffused cluster
of solo betweens, whether
never to be refused by
further forest mass or not

2

Crouched between trees, pardonably elongated, and whatever a like surpassing can't withstand of its own bareness of relation. Instead of occlusion there can be primary barring that lightens the chequer of elation gone freely down radiants between. Attuning the monotone (given) how such brisk striations become (scarcely) extended into origin, browsing frieze by a lightsome straddle of gift. Under ontological flak steep-ribbed origin now how flicker-some, slightens any disparaging of unsilted light only a branch away from resorptive mediation. Whatever void gets sipped by implements in branches spreading their tracts on spend it scarce: parings of universal cross-pleat would be slippery at evading interruption if this genus didn't offer it rebar, now fretted to a tree's frontispiece in microarmature. What is between branches isn't the question of their being fully open. It's a hinter-face (linear visage inland of entwinement) that doesn't double back through its interspace statics but becomes trusted with exit from between. Sheetlets of sky within what blue expansion the branches can provision untearingly. Unshutter these traverses, the network will lead its internal fibre through a mild non-insulation of expectant pore. Given there was no third domain that wasn't also interceding for the asymmetric ratio itself: de-mediating is to re-originate, open such lessenings to a forest forestation where branches got themselves across the tenure without cleating. By inflection to key vector, unaimed within the frame, balmed by the simultaneities of between, combed throughward by timefracts in awe. Evergreens' deeper stellar is figured against a deciduous sparkle of sky nearest in blink for flaming at betweens, apprehensive in having no quicker take on conflagration than these slit shallows.

Unabated tree shoulder shifts its verticals between, doesn't darn these patterns for what the source contorts but films diagonals against what a stronger-ago re-ravelled. Were it not for the wrest of branch off branch avoiding perfusion the remaining conjointure couldn't keep so frictionless here. Splitting materiality open not to de-matter it but opportune a meta-dependency that does flit between, the real notch scrapes sacral across such loose conciliance of origin. In trying to collapse all the remains of scope onto one orison they won't forego how lapse into branch pleads prayer a ray at a spine across diversity, assaying among reversions. Betweens which filtrate an infinite finitude do navigate how close these branches are bound for zeros in relief, themselves the pliant commonality between poor symmetric com-passings. The least of a beyond gets fronded from its crosshatchings between. Discontinuous but refers divergence at a rate localizing betweens from such an unsewn or junctionless encrossing. Which doesn't outstain the luminous but resorts compositely at each shyest eyelet, a sky not roughed out along branch but better gested in splinters. Grist of guileless puncture graining source in counter-glances across holes in trees how close to sealant, but depth in the intervals of openness doesn't surmount. Sole host of recessive infra-leap sheers an entirety by what is yonder to it but heals the apartenance into springing up unmediably between. An other for the graft of differences to be given attributes whole lacement despite the veins broken off. Scarifying the immensity which storms through the swaying of perceptual scale: if the norms of a minimal transfer weren't crisped beyond their concentrations, branches of it couldn't repine to repair. The given in all isn't the whole to which it is given but arises off lessening the receipt-origin through to rare pores of its ownerless aspiring, privation universally relieved by moderating the receiving entirely spare at crossover. Realising the ruth of the between hasn't to embed a difficult appearance. Without a branch-cage ajar at gantries chinks could only stipulate ownership of the rifts of light or pleach blinds from a difference that overlords in disassociation by loading the swinging door. As lessened to gift otherness outsets from more than a radical, is over-complete in forwarding a finite in fretful trellis of lesion offered the premise of between. More intricate at self-dividing the grid than in remiss of beyond, suffices towards in arabesque face of. Light pecked to spots of light and singularly afforded once fording the between, nettings that wrap the beyond in an encroachability it observes until a suppler style of branching trans-defers. Singular gauze of what is credited with the frontage of its pretext, fully across. To be between branch is to proclaim it disentangled without escaping rebound on fold. Hollow crevice to be fastened remotely to passage in tube of tree, but the linings become previous branches in too much wealth of gutter to seal the dimension. A faction of branch is branch trans-partite, not immersing its middlement in hoist but protruding diagonals of what spends its gaps across the vertical. Branches divide the world more tenderly than serrated, to inject an edge's steep overstrand than in replete proof of. What is between attracts local completion of what in falling beyond serves to cross through own prior containment. The orbitant effect of a dispersal itself lapped between too accordingly to splash back over branches of rehearsals. New counters cross every fraction of the thatch, generous porous retail doesn't suspend full linear passaging by veiling the pitch. Branches have roused me to within these pores, their capillary blanks seek out a burden of uncitable nest. Branch-toss as incentive to a presence put before bars of itself, plenitude by a percentage of origin sliding its entire delves, latticing a counter-absence scarcer for its segments of collection. Cast the fewings of what comes to be (fully horizoned) a longer accompanied canopy through. To be holed repletedly but between stark admittances, a community of tree attaining pitch of gap from its separables' selection of union. Nurturable focal pin deriving deep seam from what in itself was never obliquely branch-woven. Branches can't plait themselves out of the way until key flaking key is what a strikable openness has, an ovule at the interspersal gain. Repartition (a plenitude) bears out the way branches crouch forward of their gift of intersection, tailing the multiple until all is exact inaction before a plural revision in sight of ransoms. Given by another fountain than going apart, driven along the indemnifying distraint of branch. To be so lush for original gift unless dilating at minimal pole betweenwhiles: coming to be that a time has become the shared trans-erectives of unfused lattice more original than itself. Letting the more than completable come between each least co-angle of branch. Slight adjuncts tense enough for horizon to need no better-favoured web than this. So easily between it de-middles what it is on behalf of, slights will unclot any disclosives beyond the whole. Already sheltered but not needing to be let in, each node will future its unswollen universal at a budding between. Tree meaning these insets aren't rival attachments to a diaspora of places but lends the semi-segments a sphincter at the between. If this is against inattentive horizon, between-branch doesn't clasp any counter-attempt, reclusions like these are transitory lengths of the entwinement's own delay. The more earth throws closedness between, the less that space desponds in kind, its petty wrap poorly constant but attentive to the interfruct of the least demeanour of origin reserving 'out' the mediation. Serving origin-excess at its weaker enclave, less with interploy than enter it unmade. If the striation can be richly replenished it is at a locally stood-down hindrance which retains its own stricter less, a beyond not resectored-to but be-stirring this mesh through.

3

Bifurcation flown to a gift of between with no farther petition off looming fields

adjacency stances edging across the clearfell light

a dissimilarity value between branches only if there is sheer skeletal outreach in the target saming it

greater than an expanse of person wishing to pass between branches that keep open, lost to maintenance, the scarcity of origin

hinterland dome zooming between branches seen to be no frailer than the pruning of ground

unconditional in ramification but corrected to the distances that come in for their apartnesses between

nets ceaselessly crossed without being pierced: betweens already hollow, branch-pieces have no harsher trawling to do

acute singles performing (open score) between branches and knots

branch-shiver on braid which is an unknit environing since no discharge of transects was given in the between itself branches grow differentially across what is theirs concurrently, the interspaces are currency in a while for the exchange of apart

fill the race between branches with no coiling of what out-unfolded them, unrounding spaces must clear sparsely between

the tree has a definite no to levels of branching, its lean bevel once round corners deserves dipping or rising fully enough for betweens

not a flake of horizon to set before the veering flick of branch: the quick of tree stakes out this diagonal about-quake

post-interventionally sidebranches might become permanently occluded but badly placed branch will reprove crossing them out of the between

forelimbs by re-attiring the gradient, full retroactive adjacency but rarely inwoven

branches do plain overlap, slap against the between, won't texture their way to a blindly knotted open for too many beginnings in the midst of self-spun avoidal voids

(branches that haven't spent out a deform of corrugated support on their recoilless betweens)

narrow angle between branches attracts a wider unjoining at the weakness of tracery off serried shingle

such beakless betweens still read from the rostrum of distance, returning it closer than the immediate hollows vacantly sure of across between through light beyond branch, stemming in gift but attracting the reft into received hollow

tenses of verticality taken whole whilst spanning the diagonals of between-branch

trans-able ramified blank shot heavily, a counter-discharge at so much reverted gap

where all attention is tip-driven, the mechanism for the decision to form a branch is unknown, so let whatever freestream sees an amplitude spare a between

irony's harms show a vocation for shuttering the intimacy, but not astoundable between festoons of clattered innocence enough

remote swirling between uncurls out of its sortal distance, a free intolerance of sky to any other segment of itself bar this

could containment be so through-construed (as this) in any other storm of assemblage?

to own nothing between but not live out such inter-extensions admitted as a wanderer

earth spans our traversing throughout the filters hiding it from relocation, unless protection opts for transfer by slender betweens

dripping the between onto its diverticular heart as if asperged pro-versely, not dispersing it from an adverse apprising of resurgence nothing draws near but what is distinct between, it counts that collateral recession no separation

a between is not evenly a shrunk component, there is no capture of any detriment to distance except within its linkage onto uninterrupted traversity

trans as in light parrying, co-induces a star voluminously at each brighter filter-point

angular divergence across strong leaches of sky not becoming inward to the web, but its crossing starches

exacting unstarkly whatever other logistic has mapped laterally impotent amenity on disallowed but integral space

the soul of departure no retreatant from the physical aperture of a between

a plurality of deferent counter-weaves staying put (through) once the tense of diverting between is the perfect fore of deep branch

not what ventilates branch unless eventuating in the between a fore-draught of uninfesting reserve

where a local between becomes dispersive of the permit to gap, rehearsing retractile earth a tree's hip away from such hollow vault

what is between suspects a sleight by adhesion adjoining but can't consecrate to the uninnocence of life, must intake free of any pains of interval not threshed by branch relief all we can know from this lacing (unsheened stances of light) is the much of it really *toward* what might be a revealed indifferent becomes the resurrect naturalism

something already hollow enough of us to have it criss-cross indivisions never sheerly in bisection but a sharpness of betweens beside, splaying out on empty but reprovided against itself

between branches the safety reticulation of the world is driven too far forward for consoling its pre-existence meshlessly

supple crossings of a world sensible within this abstention between branches, though its spares (spheres) still circulate unculled

when you try to leave this little span take with you from the tips the lenities of such diagonalised bridging

unwoven distances pine for a thread between creases, outbedded so far as it does sheetly returns by branch: thinness of horizon shall recuperate its parings handled (entrusted) at the moment of slice recognition

between branches a willing city peers into the derision it makes abhor to the green narrows, then grows huger in fear of the counter-decisions of itself

two or more branches scarcely clip their frontline once going apart, but to an ossuary of sidebranches: what they striate three-dimensionally is no calculus of cleft but one unnumbered agenda of adjacency

a magnitude of root crag between branches, the wrap diagonal doesn't offer to enweb horizon but is voice to arboreal escape paths gently relagging the median of release length jitter bears on the green graphic of outstem, distalic the diagonal service of under-limb to swerve italic

idyllic encrustment rough-shingles the tracery, appears sharply spent but spearlessly through to what would commingle smoothly aside by any other insulation

friendly completion between branch encourages devolvement of a dilation for the omitted on behalf of

never a scarf encoding vision but rare enough for a tilted scarp of holes corroding incision

branches counter-stabbing between but to within diurnal staffage: diagonal wrap of vertical slippage into accompaniment

fetches between what ample branch didn't stretch, the texture pitches neither fore nor rear but is filtrated diagonally, a domained scarcity-to ahead of any climax of surface

between branch intimates how the re-scenery co-sends in gap, that of trans-tending it a deferent scrap of clothed tree

profuse around branch crossings not drawn into but porous before gaps lacking the hubs of absence: reach apart to a different (non-aberrant) insecurity of dependence

least stances an out-of-requital between duly: the behalf which is branch for gap by sakes porous of dispensation ornament?

Acknowledgements

'Slights Agreeing Trees' was first published by Prest Roots 2, 2002.

I am grateful to the following magazines where some of these texts in extract first appeared:

> *Axolotl, Blackbox Manifold, Chicago Quarterly, Denver Quarterly, Ecopoetics, Fragmente, Free Verse, The Gig, Gists and Piths, Intercapillary Space, Masthead, Poetry Wales, Quarterly West Magazine, Salt Magazine, Shearsman, Stride, Warwick Review.*

Nate Dorward offered invaluable initial support to this collection and I remain indebted for his design input while expressing my grateful obligation to Tony Frazer for bringing this project to fruition.

I should also like to thank these individuals for support, advice and friendship: John Allitt†, Anthony Barnett, Tilla Brading, Mark Dickinson, Chris Goode, Matthew Hall, Edmund Hardy, Geoffrey Hartman, Louise Ho, D.S. Marriott, Anthony Mellors, Candice Ward†, Tom West, Lissa Wolsak.

I am particularly grateful to Simon Lewty for his frontispiece.

www.ingramcontent.com/pod-product-compliance
Lightning Source LLC
Chambersburg PA
CBHW022010160426
43197CB00007B/360
* 9 7 8 1 8 4 8 6 1 2 4 2 6 *